RUNNING
REWIRED

REINVENT YOUR RUN
FOR STABILITY,
STRENGTH, & SPEED

2nd Edition

JAY DICHARRY

VELO
press

CrossFit® is a registered trademark of CrossFit, Inc.
Ironman® is a registered trademark of World Triathlon Corporation

an imprint of Ulysses Press
PO Box 3440
Berkeley, CA 94703
www.velopress.com

VeloPress is the leading publisher of books on sports for passionate and dedicated athletes around the world. Focused on cycling, triathlon, running, swimming, nutrition/diet, and more, VeloPress books help you achieve your goals and reach the top of your game.

ISBN: 978-1-64604-652-2
Library of Congress Control Number: 2023951682

Printed in Korea
10 9 8 7 6 5 4 3 2 1

Cover design: Kevin Roberson
Cover photograph: Tim De Frisco
Interior design: Anita Koury
Interior layout: what!design @ whatweb.com
Interior photographs: Jeff Clark + Lane Pearson
Illustrations: Charlie Layton
Editors: Renee Jardine, Renee Rutledge
Proofreader: Sherian Brown
Index: Beverlee Day
Location courtesy of Kevin Boss, Boss Sports Performance

To my kids: My future is happier with you.

To my wife, who always looks for the positive.

To my parents, for providing support and opportunity.

To my mentors, who pushed me.

To my friends, who let me be myself.

To chocolate, for being delicious.

To our planet, the ultimate playground: We'll protect you.

To the musicians of my hometown, NOLA: Your music moves us.

CONTENTS

THE RUNNING REWIRED PROGRAM

Setting Yourself Up for Success

There's that feeling that you get after you crush a workout, hit a new PR on race day, or beat your friend to the top of the local hill or high alpine peak. It's a feeling of success . . . and it feels good, really good. We thrive on challenge and train in pursuit of this feeling of success. Every runner knows that it takes a lot of hard work to get there. But a lot of runners get confused by this concept: They end up interpreting "a lot of hard work" to mean "a high volume of work." In the quest to log the miles it's easy to lose sight of the quality of those miles. First place isn't awarded to the person who racks up the highest weekly mileage or trains the hardest. Instead, medals adorn the necks of those who nail the fundamentals, which in turn allows them to train consistently and successfully. You've got to put in the miles to get fit, but how can you be sure that your training is setting you up for success? Put simply, there are things that all runners of all abilities should be doing outside running to improve their running. If you want to run better, you need to move better.

Discussions about "running better" invariably seem to lead to the topic of form, but before we go there let's take a step back and look at reality. How you run is an expression of you and your experience. You probably aren't a Tarahumara native, and you probably aren't a Kenyan. We all envy the perfect posture, leg drive, and effortlessly springy gait of these runners. That idealized stride wasn't a result of being born at elevation or bestowed with great genetics—it was built through skilled movement. It was lifestyle that wired these runners' bodies for postural alignment and efficient muscle recruitment, first as children playing in the field, later working in those fields, and eventually through a lot of hard training that led them to beat the entire field. If we consider how a lifestyle structured around physical activity and progressive running factors in, it's not the case that the Kenyan and Tarahumara cultures are "born to run"; rather, their bodies have "adapted to run." Conversely, it should come as no surprise that our own lifestyle, built around modern conveniences and topped off with a bunch of running, doesn't produce the same results.

Training to move better

Movement skill is critical. Athletes competing in ball sports spend the bulk of their time training their bodies to move better. Through practice they build a strategy that can be put to use every time they step onto the turf, field, or court. They know how to execute good form before the first ball is put into play. Fighter pilots refine their reflexes until they reach a point where they can fly intuitively. Your 105-pound neighbor can nail yoga poses you've only seen in pictures, not because she's strong, but because she's skilled. You don't step into the huddle, into a cockpit, or into a one-handed handstand on the yoga mat until you have a baseline of skill preparation. Likewise, highly efficient runners have mastered the skill of running.

The legendary running coach Joe Vigil once said, "It's hard being a running coach because the kids who show up for practice are highly motivated, but they are the same kids that lacked the athleticism to make the team in [insert sport-of-choice]." These kids are steeped in the promise that work ethic can beat talent given enough time and determination—they get out of bed, lace up their shoes, and run. Sometimes they run easy, sometimes hard, and sometimes even harder. Many of them end up running themselves into the ground, missing peak potential, or worse yet, missing training due to injury. But harder doesn't mean better, and volume doesn't make champions.

There are specific skills that you should have in your running toolbox. The repetitive nature of running means that many of us take a body that really doesn't know how to move at its best and rack up the mileage. Through years of repetition you wire your body to move one way and run one way. Then when someone comes along and tells you that you need to improve your form, or move a different way, you can't simply do what they are saying. You haven't built the muscle memory to move differently. Even subtle changes to your running form feel awkward and hard. You can't help but notice that your form still looks nothing like that of the Kenyans. And your times aren't improving. A lot of runners have conducted this experiment and failed, concluding that focusing on form is a waste of time. Well, there is a better way to run better.

It starts with this little secret: Your body drives your running form. The old adage says "form follows function." Likewise, running form follows body function. Running better requires you to move better. Under stress. Under fatigue. And under the hot sun with your archrival breathing down your neck. In these moments, you don't have the luxury of going over an eight-point mental checklist on running form and body awareness. You should have learned that routine a long time ago. If not, that time begins now.

Think about where you are right now as a runner, and where you'd like to be. Everyone wants running to feel smooth, efficient, and less stressful. To hit that goal requires you to train in a way that is more well rounded and more *athletic*—but always with the intention of specifically improving your running. We are all busy, and adding more to what you are already doing can seem like a big ask. But this process will be fun, because you'll feel yourself improving in ways you've never experienced. We'll explore specific strategies to improve your movement and re-invent your run.

A study of one

The science of training is evolving. It's only been in the past 20–30 years that we have had access to the tools and technology to further our understanding of the body and create progress in sports science. Now we have labs to do research, people with lots of letters behind their names, and coaches who are hungry to find better ways for their athletes to train. The field of performance science is constantly evolving, and its recent discoveries have been implemented in this new edition of *Running Rewired*. And what difference has this innovation made? Records are falling faster than rain. Look at any sport and you'll see a sharp spike in performance gains over the past three decades. Decades ago, people just ran. When we found out how effective intervals are at improving physiological performance capacity, they became standard practice. Theory changes. Science changes. And if you harness this knowledge and change your training, ultimately your running times can change.

There are a few things you need to know to get more out of the science on training. First, it remains the case that most of the research on running is focused on injury prevention, and there's been a definitive evolution in how we treat running injuries in recent years. We have better information, which means you can have better results. But when we survey the research on running performance, we face a harder task. Most of the running performance studies involve either elite runners or college kids who play video games for several hours a day and get bonus points for showing up to be a research subject. Unless you are an elite runner or a couch-potato college student, these results may not accurately apply to you. To evolve running performance, we need to look comprehensively at the research being done both inside and outside of running. The fields of biomechanics research, motor control, generalized strength and conditioning research, and yes, even bodybuilding make up a vast body of research that translates to running performance. We will draw on this science to learn how to move better.

To be effective, research needs to be translated to your individual needs. In my work as a physical therapist and researcher, I consider each runner as a unique case study. I begin by asking a simple question: How can I set up this runner for success? It's my job to pinpoint problems that cause those running ouches and plug the holes in a runner's performance potential. I've conducted musculoskeletal examinations and high-tech gait lab assessments on thousands of runners in my career. While this book is no substitute for a one-on-one running gait lab examination, there is a pattern to the problems that plague runners. I can say with confidence that you will benefit from fixing your own imbalances to ensure that you put the best you into every run. I've taken advantage of the research that's out there, along with my own observations, and conducted some of my own

tests in the lab to see what kind of efforts build more durable and better runners. I know that if I can give you the tools to create a more durable body that can resist the stress of running, you can push the boundaries of your own physical performance.

Running versus practicing

It obviously takes time and practice to refine your craft. In his book *Outliers*, Malcolm Gladwell explains the theory that it takes 10,000 hours of practice to be the best. It's human nature to zero in on the total amount of time practiced and start logging the hours. This is a big mistake, particularly when it comes to running. If you don't know how to move better right from the start, you'll end up doing the same thing over and over again, expecting a different result. Practicing the same thing repeatedly just reinforces your current movement patterns. Adding more volume of less-than-perfect movement means you get really good at moving poorly. What you practice and how you practice it makes all the difference. To run better we have to realize that running is a skill. And skilled running stems from practicing skilled movement.

Gladwell's book was largely based on the work of psychologist Anders Ericsson, who categorized practice as purposeful and deliberate. Purposeful practice is kind of like running. Your training plan tells you to run, so you run. You keep logging more volume, heartbeats, and mileage in your black box in pursuit of a certain goal, but the target is usually set on a specific time or distance. This approach doesn't exactly make you a better runner. You don't get better at running in a way that avoids injury. You don't optimize your stride to your full performance potential. Instead, you keep turning up the volume, hoping to hear that magic song that inspires you to a new PR. Most runners just want to run, but that's not likely to make you better at running. And that's where a different type of practice comes in.

We need to drill down on what helps people get better. Ericsson describes deliberate practice as doing a specific task with the intent of improving performance. To get better at running, you must first understand the sport so you can identify the sport-specific skills that are critical to improving. Then, you need a formal plan of attack to develop those skills. And then there's ongoing focus to continue to improve and refine those skills. For a runner, deliberate practice entails taking specific actions to improve durability and economy, and this doesn't always involve running.

> Stop defining your net worth by your race times and weekly mileage. Start focusing on improving quality movement.

Instead of asking you to run more, I'm asking you to start a plan to move better. With deliberate practice the neurophysiology in your brain will adapt and rewire its strategy for running. We'll tackle the what, why, and how to change your body and improve your movement so you can be a more durable runner and increase your capacity to run efficiently. We will build your proficiency at these skills, effectively rewiring how your body moves so you can run better. It's a big promise, and it does require a commitment from you: You will need to fit at least two additional workouts into your weekly training schedule.

I know your time is valuable. If a lack of time is your primary obstacle, I will reassure you that it's well worth the investment. Virtually every runner I've ever met would be better served shortening a run, or even dropping it entirely, and adding some skill work. If you've got the time, simply add this plan on top of your running.

Maybe you are still unconvinced. But what if I told you that it's possible to craft a body that moves well, under control, in the most efficient way possible? Imagine what it would feel like to develop a running gait that is more symmetrical and less stressful, reducing fatigue to keep you feeling fresh all season. The promise of improved joint health and faster running times is hard to resist.

This program will get you results. It was a daunting task to take training plans from individual runners I've worked with over the years and scale them to the masses, but it works. Since the first publication of *Running Rewired* I've received thousands of emails from runners and coaches across the globe touting the results they've earned following the plan from the first edition. It's incredibly humbling. Going into this new edition, I can attest that new runners, seasoned runners, high school teams, collegiate teams, run clubs, and elite training centers have successfully adopted this plan. No matter where you are now, this plan can scale and grow with you. And this new edition and updated plan will push your understanding, consistency, and progress further still. There are no shortcuts to get you there. But if you are ready to invest some hard work and be consistent with your training, this plan will bring you success. Research shows us that people stick to plans when they understand "the why." Let's learn more about what happens to you as you run, and how the Running Rewired program will take you and your running to the next level.

Think Backward to Run Forward

We all need to be students of our sport. For some of us, it's been a while since we sat in a classroom. But you can probably recall that being a successful student requires that you know what's going to be on the test. When you know that much, you know how to prepare and what to study. Well, class is in session: What does running test?

When you run, each stride tests your body. If we understand the specific problems or challenges that we face as runners we can work backward from there and establish a plan to be better prepared. I'm sure you'd be happier with an A on your running report card, right? Let's look at what you need to do to prepare your body to run better—the right work done at the right time and in the right dose—to maximize your results.

WHAT REALLY HAPPENS WHEN YOU RUN

The thrill of running can distract us from the reality of what is happening to the body with every stride. Your heart beats harder, pumping blood throughout the body. Sweat drips down your forehead as your body temperature rises. You feel the wind on your face as you turn round the track, up the trail, or down the road. These are the images that running conjures up in our heads and they are real, but while your heart and lungs are driving your engine toward redline, your chassis is under a lot of stress. Like it or not, your body must deal with 2.5–3 times its body weight with every single stride. Think about this for a minute. If you stand up on both legs, you have half your body weight on each leg. And if you stand on one leg, that's 100 percent of your body weight on one leg. Now take a barbell, add about 150 percent of your body weight to it, and hoist the load up and onto your shoulders; then stand on one leg. Like it or not, this

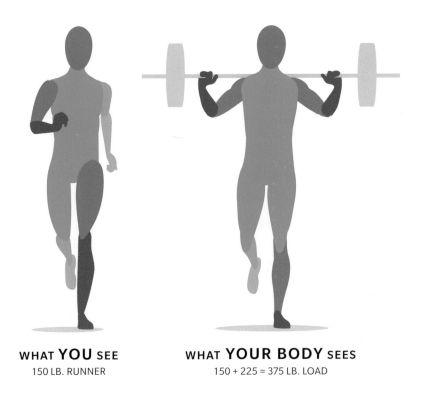

WHAT YOU SEE
150 LB. RUNNER

WHAT YOUR BODY SEES
150 + 225 = 375 LB. LOAD

FIGURE 1.1 The Real Load of Running
Running demands mechanical work. In a fraction of a second, you need to lift a significant load up and forward while maintaining control. You can't change the reality of running, but you can prepare for it.

is how much stress your bones, tendons, muscles, cartilage, and ligaments support with every single stride you take. As runners, we've been told that distance running is a small amount of stress applied to your body for a long period of time. Well, we just shot that idea into oblivion. If anything, we could say that running is large stresses acting on our body for a long time.

Further complicating matters, running isn't just a single-plane sport. In addition to these vertical forces, we also have to deal with braking and acceleration forces that amount to 40–50 percent of our body's weight. And that's while our body is kicked laterally by forces of around 15 percent body weight just from the effort of running. Running creates huge amounts of stress that act on the body from all sides with each and every step. No wonder running is hard!

This load acting on your body is absolute and somewhat mechanical. But your body's response isn't just mechanical. Imagine a rubber ball. If you throw a rubber ball off the roof, it will first accelerate to the ground. When it collides with the ground, the energy of the impact will flatten the ball out a bit and then the ball will rebound off the ground and spring back up again. The ball is passive—it compresses and rebounds based on the density of the rubber from which it is made. This is a simple illustration of how a passive object responds to load. Now imagine you are soaring through the air in mid-stride and the same gravity that accelerated the rubber ball takes you back to earth. That's where the similarity ends, because the

FIGURE 1.2 Forces at Work When You Run
Running hits your bones, muscles, and tendons with large amounts of force—it's critical to control these forces.

body isn't passive. It's a complex system of parts with a neuromuscular system that actively moves, adjusts, and coordinates these parts in response to the mechanical forces of running.

YOUR MOVEMENT SYSTEM

There are three basic systems that you use for active movement. You have joint structures, muscles, and a brain. Alone, these parts can do nothing, and together they can break world records.

Joint structures: The mechanical parts of your body are like doors and hinges. Your bones have structure, and each of these bones connects to other bones through a joint. The joints are lined with cartilage, a cool material that cushions and lubricates the bones as they move, and the bones are connected by ligaments, which tie one bone to the other. All of these support parts are important, but they are just passive pulleys and levers. That is, they can't move on their own. Doors and hinges don't move on their own either.

Muscles: This is where the work gets done. To get the door to open on its hinge requires a force to open or close it. Muscles provide this force generation for our body. They allow one joint to move on another or stabilize a joint while motion occurs somewhere else.

Brain: We have joints that provide structure, and we've got muscles that create force to move the joints, but we need something to tell those parts to move. This is where your brain comes in. Actually, it's not just your brain, but your entire nervous system. Think of it as a computer that is wired to a network of muscles. But the

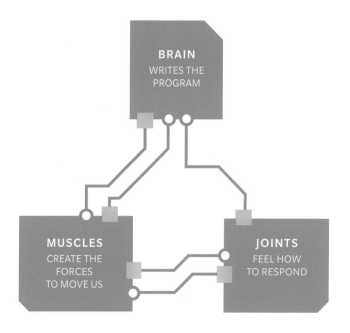

FIGURE 1.3 A Movement System Wired for Control
What's the lesson here? Joints don't provide active stability. Muscles do—and the brain pulls the trigger.

incredible thing about our nervous system is that it's not just an on/off switch. It modulates the force we create. When your brain tells your muscles to generate force to open the door, your brain adjusts how much force is needed based on the weight of the door, whether it's dragging on the carpet, or if it's sticking in the doorjamb. This amount of control allows us not just to move, but to move with precision.

better body input = better output

With each and every stride, these systems all talk to each other. The mechanical load accelerating you down to earth stimulates a chain of events. While your joints can't move on their own, they can sense compression and movement. They send signals out to your neuromuscular system, calling for action. Your brain triggers the muscles to generate a certain amount of force at just the right time. Your muscles get this message and do the work they were told. They pull on the joints to create motion. And then there's cross talk among the parts as well. Your muscles sense a change in length and relay info to your brain to make sure that you don't strain them. The joints relay information to your brain since the amount of muscle force they need changes as they arc through their range of motion. This cross talk is essentially a system of checks and balances to make sure

things are going well. If done correctly, your body produces a net mechanical force that is just enough to counter the mechanical load trying to squash you down like a pancake. If all goes well, you just took one single stride. Nice job. Now all you have to do is sustain this for several thousand strides on today's run.

PROGRAMMING QUALITY MOVEMENT

These three systems run a program over and over with each stride you take. Each element in the system has specific inputs and outputs to modify the *quality* of your stride. This is what's missing from our understanding of running. Runners have an unrelenting focus on volume. More miles per week obviously puts more mechanical load on your joints. It's the body's job to produce a controlled and efficient response, rising to the challenge and controlling your body. A poor movement program equates to poor body control. When the body becomes overwhelmed by the demands of running, it sets us up for injury or leads to compromised performance. Specifically, it is how we deal with the mechanical demands of running that dictates how well we perform. The two big questions are:

1. **Is your movement safe?** What type of movement skill and body awareness do you bring to running?

2. **Is your movement efficient?** Could you rewire the way you move to drive you forward with less effort, and less form breakdown during your runs?

An efficient movement program improves the quality of your stride for long-term joint health and efficiency. Just as we can adjust the quantity of our running volume, we can learn to improve the quality of our running volume. Your brain learns through movement and awareness to know when, how much, and how fast to drive your legs. You can improve your skills by better understanding the input your brain is receiving and rewiring your movement program to get your legs moving more safely and efficiently.

Dynamic plastic

What's my favorite thing to eat? Oatmeal chocolate chip cookies. You didn't know that 5 seconds ago, but you do now. Do you know how you learned to swim? Do you know how the brain recovers after a stroke? The answers to these questions have one thing in common: neural plasticity. Your brain is capable of learning. Not just rote memorization, but actually learning how to do new things at any age! When you learn, your brain makes new connections from one cell to another. The more you practice, the more robust these connections become. It's the old practice makes perfect thing. Your nerves are literally building skill by laying down connectivity from nerve to nerve.

The wires that connect your systems are dynamic. They adjust their signals depending on your needs. Running on asphalt, concrete, grass, and over trail irregularities present different inputs, and all require different outputs in terms of muscle action and timing. Changing pace requires modifications as well. Your nervous system makes all of the necessary adjustments behind the scenes. The same thing happens when you get a new pair of shoes—your body makes slight changes to account for the new environment your foot now sits on. All of this learning that your body does to account for these differences is evidence that it can also learn and adapt to run better. The Running Rewired program uses neural plasticity to train your body to run with more control for better durability and better performance.

Moving with precision and force

A lot of coaches will tell you that runners self-select their own efficient running form. Well, kind of. There's optimal form, which we'll call Plan A. And then there's making the best of what you've got, or Plan B. Most runners figure out how to compensate for any shortcomings in their current make-up of mobility, stability, strength, and power. In other words, your brain's ability to adapt is being hijacked by your body and its limitations. You refine and practice Plan B over years of purposeful practice. Plan B can certainly get the job done to log your miles. But I'd argue that Plan B is second rate.

It's not my intention to come at you with guns a-blazing and tell you everything you know about running is wrong, but given the fact that your brain can be rewired and your running form can actually change, why not work on recovering your own personal Plan A? Movements that feel awkward today can become instinctual. Through deliberate practice, Plan A can also become instinctual. Settle for Plan B and you will leave performance on the table because Plan B stops short of harnessing your durability or capacity.

In recent years recovery has been trending as the key to becoming a more resilient athlete. Sure, training wears you down and recovery is when your body repairs itself and you reap the rewards. But "better recovery" won't fix your imbalances. And better recovery can be exhausting given the long list of protocols: taking a supplement; jumping into a hyperbaric oxygen chamber; eating more carbs or less carbs; getting a massage, ice bath, or contrast bath; wearing another device; attending an altitude camp; and it goes on and on. These protocols are passive; things done *to you* don't integrate your brain to rewire your movement skill and strategy. These things may bring about a 0.1 percent improvement here and there, but a plan of action is more rewarding. When you are actively involved in improving the way you move, you get results.

preparation > recovery

If you have problems or injuries that affect the way you run, it's time to fix them. Take your aching back and painful knees and throw 35–50 miles a week at them, and running won't help. Neither would soccer, basketball, or ice hockey. Placing a huge load on top of existing problems only makes things worse. Your injury cycles prevent consistent training. Break the cycle. You don't need to be a freak of nature to be successful, but you do need to improve your movement quality.

There's another issue I frequently see in runners that compromises movement. Many will tell me, "I can't jump." Here's what this really means: "I can't coordinate my body well enough to deliver a solid chunk of force down to the floor to blast me up and forward against gravity." This is a big problem because this is exactly what running demands of us. In fact, research shows that people who drive more force down to the ground in a shorter period of time run faster. Period. Every runner, at every level, can train and improve this skill.

We are going to open up the black box of running and establish a system for making you a better runner. Your body drives your running form. Build a better body and you will improve your running form. By focusing on the specific skills that improve running, you can move with precision and strengthen your spring. To move with precision you need enough mobility to move unencumbered and enough stability to control the path your body takes over each mile. Building the skills of mobility and stability will reduce your "stress per stride" and ensure your body symmetry is dialed. Moving better makes you more durable as a runner, which allows your training to be more consistent. A stronger spring leads to better performance because your ability to deliver more oomph down to the ground makes for a faster stride. The Running Rewired workouts are the backbone of a step-by-step program to change your body and evolve your running.

Troubleshoot Broken Wiring

Imagine you are out on a beautiful trail run with your buddy Wes. You are talking to Wes about the vacation you are planning, but all he wants to talk about is the fact that his right IT (iliotibial) band is killing him. He tried the foam roller but that didn't help. He got a massage last week; that didn't help either. You fade back to take a look at his stride and notice that his right knee is collapsing inward. You tell Wes to steer his leg straight. But Wes has no idea how to correct this problem. So he overcompensates by forcing his knees outward. Now he's running on the outsides of his feet and that hurts his feet. Running this way feels strange, and it's much harder, and Wes becomes frustrated. The real problem is that Wes's hip is collapsing inward. Most people would think that this is due to muscle weakness, and that is a possibility. But for the vast majority of runners, there's something else entirely different going on. Systems don't work when they aren't plugged in.

Most runners' hip muscles are inhibited, or unplugged. Put simply, you can't make toast if your toaster isn't plugged in. Likewise, your hip muscles won't turn on unless you teach them to connect with your brain. Personal trainers often make the claim that heavy squats fix everything. I couldn't disagree more. Cramming more bread into a toaster that isn't plugged in won't fix the problem. Squatting with 200 pounds won't fix your issues because your body will just shift load to other muscles and continue to compensate. Likewise, if you pile running volume on top of inhibited hips, it doesn't help because running and strength aren't the problem. Your broken wiring is the problem. To plug the muscle back in, we need to teach it to work and coordinate it with the rest of the body.

Your volume isn't the problem. Your movement strategy is.

Recently a runner came to see me with hip pain. It wasn't bad enough to keep her from running, but it was consistently present. Her coach and friends had told her to strengthen her glutes, so she began going to a Butts and Guts class every week. What was the net impact after two years? Nothing—she saw zero improvement. Her strength training class couldn't fix the problem; in fact, it was throwing still more load on top of her problem. Her body had learned to cheat the movement and move more weight on the bar, but she couldn't move better. And none of the time she invested had helped her running

stride. We took a step back and cleaned up her movement problems. Within three weeks she was symptom-free and set a PR in the half-marathon. When she returned to those classes, she had better movement and she could see the results. When you move correctly, you move at your best. And most importantly, your body learns skills that improve your running.

DON'T SETTLE FOR PLAN B

Good runners have a gait that is instinctively smooth. With each stride, brain and body deliver an optimal stride. These athletes have trained to develop a "Plan A" strategy to move and run as efficiently as they can. Runners look to the elites for advice on how to improve their own form. It's frustrating when putting advice into action doesn't play out so well when the foot hits the ground. Let's take a step back and look at how our bodies learn to move, and how your own learned movements may be the biggest block to realizing your best run. For best results, we have to practice quality movement, but the quality of your correct movement is only as good as your body allows it to be.

Case in point: Our friend Wes would like to clean up his gait. But he doesn't bring a perfect body to running. And his work lifestyle doesn't help. He sits on planes for more hours at a stretch than some people sleep at night, and then he sits more in meetings all day. Sitting can corrupt posture, effectively shutting off or inhibiting the core and hip muscles. Also, Wes has an old injury that makes his right ankle joint stiff. The tightness in his hips prevents him from getting a good push-off so his leg swings farther in front of his body and less behind. This shift in stride overworks the muscles around the knee, so that they're not capable of steering the leg straight, and that makes running more stressful on his body. And the stiffness in his right ankle shifts him to the outside of his foot with each and every step, which imparts yet more wobble to the path of his leg swinging through space.

Wes wants to improve his control while running. But with so many factors at work, his body has resorted to Plan B. Wes has adapted to his problems by jerry-rigging his gait. Wes is not the only one—evolution has programmed us to figure out the most energy-efficient way to walk and run. Wes's body has compensated and rewired his gait reflex to make it as efficient as possible within his body's current limitations. The body gets good at what it practices, and with each run, Wes continued to engrain a compensated gait thanks to his stiff ankle and unplugged hips.

And then one day, Wes sought some help from his friend at the gym. He got all sorts of advice to help improve motion, and after a few months' time, his hip and ankle motion improved a lot. But Wes's running form didn't change a bit. Why? You can have better mobility, but your body has to know how to use it. It takes practice to integrate new movement into your brain's programming. If you want to do that, you've got to rewire the way you move.

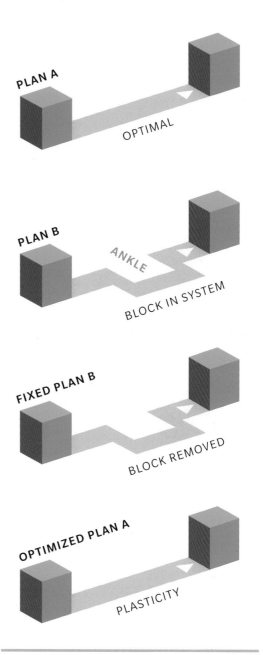

FIGURE 2.1 Practice Equals Plasticity
Motion blocks force you to move a different way. Once a block is removed, you must practice skilled control in the new movement to see improvement in your run.

REWIRING REFLEXIVE MOVEMENT

Scratch your nose. It's easy—just do it right now. What happened? You read a command. Your brain agreed. It sent a message to the muscles in your arm to lift your hand, bring it to your face, precisely find the location on your face where the nose is, and wiggle the fingers to create movement and scratch. That's a lot

BRAIN
VOLUNTARY
MOVEMENTS

MODIFY

SPINAL CORD
REFLEXIVE
EVENTS

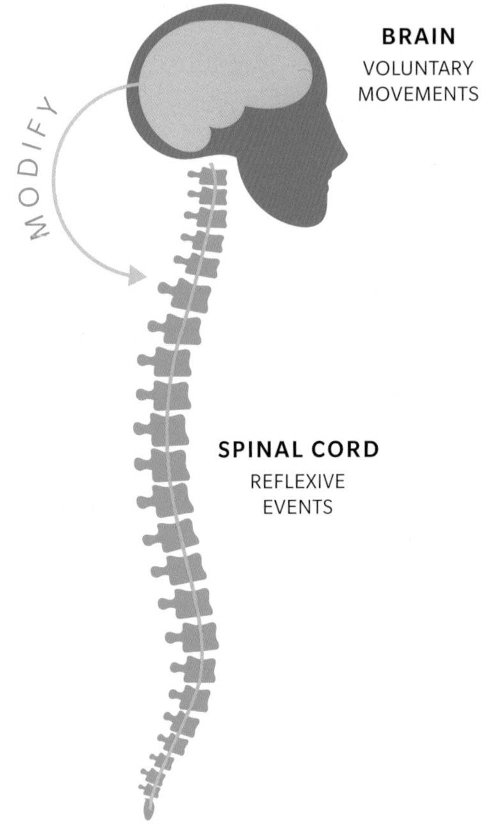

FIGURE 2.2 Subconscious Running
The instructions for your running gait come from the central pattern generators, which are just below your brain.

of steps just to scratch your nose, isn't it? All of this occurred through something called voluntary movement. You made a conscious decision to move and your brain carried out the task.

Now, get up, walk to the end of the room, and then back. Once again, your brain made a voluntary decision to give this a try. You got up and started to walk. But after that, things went very differently. With each step you flexed your hip up, extended the knee, swung the lower leg through, let a foot fall to the floor, rolled through the ankle, pushed through the calf to propel the body, and then repeated. This happened, but you didn't think through it. Gait is not voluntary, but rather reflexive.

Reflexive movements occur without conscious thought. In fact, the signals that bounce around your body telling you to crawl, walk, and run are carried out by a special program called your central pattern generators, or CPGs. The key thing to understand is that these CPGs are located under the brain in the spinal cord, and this is why gait doesn't require focused brainpower. Since conscious thought originates in our brain, in a way, it's like running in your subconscious. Every step you take reinforces your gait pattern, whether it's best for you or not. Sometimes aches and pains you've accumulated along your running career result in a limp that is noticeable to your friends, but not to you—it just feels normal. The CPGs learn from all the practice you do in a repetitive movement like gait, and practice builds connectivity. Sure, it is possible to overpower this reflex. If you want, you can push off harder on your left leg versus your right, but this would require brainpower because you would be modifying the normal reflexive pattern of gait sent out via the CPGs in your spinal cord.

This is why changing running form can be hard. Trying to hit perfect form with your less-than-perfect body results in you fighting your own movement. If you have ever tried to change your cadence, you know this firsthand. Running along at 162 steps per minute for eight years and then trying to hit 180 steps per minute will require huge effort on the part of your brain. You can't make that shift quickly. The same goes for posture. How can a runner "stand tall" for a half-marathon when she has no idea how to find a neutral spine position when she is standing still?

Still, there are plenty of running coaches out there telling people to shorten their contact time on the ground to run faster. This advice started with an experiment with a group of the best runners in the United States. They were told to shorten their contact time during all their runs, but this required completely reorganizing how hard they pushed down on each and every stride. Even though these were elite bodies, they had no idea how to actually do this and forced huge changes in muscle recruitment and intensity. It was a total disaster that resulted in every single runner being injured.

Reducing contact time will make you faster, but your body has to be trained on how to do this properly before you can expect it to integrate and improve your gait. You *can* make changes in your running form, but good form

is not going to happen in one session with one cue. Your body needs to build a database of proper muscle memory. Once your body has "been there" it can easily find its way back, just like riding a bike.

BUILDING MUSCLE MEMORY

When Wes came to see me we found out that his external rotators, which are responsible for steering the hips, were unplugged. Through treatment, Wes learned how to feel and engage his hip muscles through a very isolated movement. Initially, he couldn't carry a conversation while doing it—while not hard physically, he found it tremendously difficult mentally. For most of us, the mental concentration needed to engage in a new movement ranks around 7 on a scale of 1 to 10. This is the cognitive stage of improving movement. During this stage, movement is not smooth and requires lots of brainpower. And at this early stage of the game, the cue "steer the leg straight" doesn't typically work. Wes just doesn't have the muscle memory necessary to add this new skill to his gait reflex program.

Two weeks of exercises later, Wes was moving his hip more smoothly—he had laid down a few new wires. It was time to incorporate some of the movements he had practiced to become more of a full-body movement. Now when Wes is cued to steer his hips straight, he does it correctly. Instead of turning his knees out so his weight is on the outside of his foot, he maintains a strong, planted foot and moves properly from the hips. Wes feels that this movement is more correct, but it still takes some extra thought and requires a bit more work to run this way. Wes doesn't have a large mental database of correct movement. His Plan B still feels normal, and Plan A feels forced. Remember, running is reflexive. For Wes to modify his form, he has to coordinate extra input from the brain into his normal gait pattern to control his body position while running. This is now called the associative phase of improving movement. Wes can move properly on command, but the movement is not quite fully rewired.

COGNITIVE

ASSOCIATIVE

AUTONOMOUS

A month into practicing the movement, Wes finds the exercise easy—almost automatic. And it shows. This is the autonomous phase. His muscles are firing, and Wes has learned to coordinate this movement into his gait. His hip alignment when running is symmetrical. He is extending his hips correctly and his pain is completely gone. We fixed a neuromuscular problem through neuromuscular training.

Let's recap. Wes was running in pain with visible issues with his running form. The collapse of his leg was creating shear on the outside of the knee, which made his IT band angry. But what was the underlying problem that caused his leg to collapse? We know it wasn't muscle weakness—it takes about 6–8 weeks for muscles to enlarge (hypertrophy) and produce more force, and Wes was better off in just four weeks. So what happened?

Wes's leg crashed inward because the muscles in his hips that stabilize and move the joint were unplugged from his CPGs. Consequently, he couldn't steer his hip straight even if you told him how to fix it. Moving with precision requires coordinated movement—both *intra*- and *inter*muscular coordination.

Intramuscular coordination is how a muscle talks to itself. A muscle is made up of lots of fibers that shorten together to produce a muscle contraction that creates movement. When the muscle is inhibited, or unplugged, not enough of these fibers get the signal to engage. To fix this, it takes very specific, even sometimes isolated, movements to train the fibers within the muscle to talk to each other for more uniform contraction. This type of training targets muscle intelligence.

Intermuscular coordination is how muscles talk to each other. You can train like a body builder and do eight sets on the leg extension machine, improving your intramuscular coordination and strength until your quads can't fit into your

FIGURE 2.3 Strength Training for System Intelligence
The knee extension machine can produce intramuscular gains in isolated muscle strength, but more functional movements, such as the single-leg squat, build intermuscular strength and coordination to improve your run.

jeans, but fixing one muscle won't help you run any better. In sports, muscles don't act in isolation the way they do on the leg extension machine—you need to train movements, not muscles. This type of training targets system intelligence.

Some people view intermuscular coordination and the work involved as crosstraining, but this couldn't be further from the truth. Research shows that neuromuscular training delivers excellent results—reducing your risk of injury and improving coordination, speed, agility, vertical jump, and contact times. This work is complementary to your running. Crosstraining describes the work runners do to keep their hearts and lungs in shape in the absence of running volume. Complementary

training refines your skills and makes you a better runner.

When we say muscles are unplugged, we mean they are unplugged from your default reflexive movement. This is why we focus on building coordination both within and between muscles. Through practice, neural plasticity allows us to plug these precision movements into our CPGs and convert them to autopilot for precision running form.

Coordination, control, and precision are all skills that every runner needs to practice. These movements require high volume and little resistance. These skills should be practiced a couple of times every week, all season long, to ensure that the movement skill can be put to use while running. You need to own the movement. Not just in an exercise or drill, not just at mile 1, not just at mile 5. But at every repeat of your track workout, every hill effort, and every mile of your race. The end goal is to make that refined movement awareness reflexive. This is critical on race day when you need to execute the program you've practiced so many times over without spending your brainpower.

PLUG IN YOUR BRAIN

Improving skilled control in your body requires *focus*. In high school, I tried to sleep with my notebook under my pillow in hopes that some of that information would make its way into my brain. It never did. Focus is critical to learning. Neural plasticity is the process of learning where your brain creates new pathways to get information into and out of your nervous system. In short, it teaches your nerves to communicate better so that you can do things better.

To build that *skill*, your brain needs to focus on your brain-body connection. If you are training while distracting yourself with TV, social media, or your kid's homework, you are not focused. The "secret sauce" chemicals (a.k.a., neurotransmitters) aren't released to trigger your nerves to network. Your body might be moving, but you really aren't *learning*, and the outcome of that session is wasted.

When you focus on the task at hand, you will get a very different outcome. It's like turning the garden hose on full blast! You effectively flood and activate your nerves with that secret sauce of neurotransmitters (i.e., acetylcholine and epinephrine). This chemical change in your neurophysiology builds new physical networks, creates new pathways, and ensures you learn your new skill much more quickly.

Here's the takeaway: The experiences that you pay super-close attention to are what pave the way for plasticity to build better control in your body. And plasticity leads to better results.

Practice intention + focus

The following tips will help you build running skills. This is not the same as trying to do more or heavier squat reps. That's an effort to increase the load on your body to build stronger parts. *There is a place for that work*, but developing skill isn't about strength. *It's about strategy.* By practicing sport-specific movements with intent and focus, you can get the most out of *any* training you do to learn new things.

More short sessions are better than fewer long sessions: When your brain is fresh, you can challenge it a bit more. Instead of doing skill training once a week for 45 minutes, break it up into 10- to 20-minute sessions and practice 2–4 times each week. This strategy reduces fatigue and improves processing in your brain. This results in fewer errors, and more importantly, better transfer of the skill into life and sport. And it's why the *precision workouts are broken up into 15–20 minute sessions.*

Practice variability: In this plan, there are multiple exercises that solve each movement skill problem. Why? You need some variability to optimize skill. Don't just do the same three exercises each week. You'll learn more by doing *different* exercises and cycling through them.

Take breaks: Breaks are good. Rest is good. If you get super fatigued and sloppy, you are practicing and reinforcing bad form. Give yourself a short break when needed (even 15–30 seconds may be enough) to ensure you get *quality* out of each rep.

Dial down distraction

Some people love to listen to music when training, studying, or doing anything, really. But how does music impact focus? We know there's a zone of *optimal arousal*. When you pop out of bed tired in the morning, you aren't ready for the most intense concentration of your day. Likewise, slamming two cans of Red Bull and hitting the field with 100,000 fans cheering your name is likely to get you a bit too pumped up to think clearly.

poor arousal = poor outcomes

Think of music as a way to get you "into the zone." Just like Rage Against the Machine is not the right choice for writing a term paper, you aren't going to listen to Joni Mitchell if you are trying to get pumped up for your key race. When it comes to the impact of music on focus, the research is clear: If you want to use music, find something that helps to get you in the right level of mental arousal, but isn't too distracting. And if you don't think you need music to find that state of mental arousal, you are likely better off without it if the task you are doing requires a lot of focus.

Sure, you can crank up Rage Against the Machine for your final set of squats, but if you are trying to build skill, it will be a bit too intense, detract your focus away from the task, and impair your learning. Focusing your brain on what's most important is how you will earn wins!

3

Mobility and Stability for Runability

It's 3:15 on a Wednesday afternoon. After sitting in class all day, our track team bounded onto the field about 5 minutes ago. To get the team moving we began with a warm-up. It's pretty easy to see that Eva, Cole, Sam, and Jack aren't squatting correctly. What we are looking for is essentially an up-and-down motion, where the ankles and knees track forward and the hips track back. However, we notice that their ankles aren't bending. The lack of motion in their ankles is causing them to cheat somewhere else. In an effort to keep their weight over their feet, each athlete shifts backward and the spine rounds into a slump at the bottom of the squat. We conclude that the stiff ankles are limiting their form and decide to send the four athletes over to the wall for a 30-second calf stretch to get their ankles moving.

When they are finished, we watch them squat again. Eva is now squatting with perfect form. But Cole, Sam, and Jack look pretty much the same.

Well, one out of four isn't bad, but we need to take a closer look at those three. We know that reflexes are only as good as the body allows them to be. In other words, the brain figures out the most efficient way to move around the problems it encounters. And any problems in the system prevent the body from moving as well as it should. Let's look at how this plays out. Sometimes, the joint won't move, and we need to figure out why it won't move—we have a hardware problem. And sometimes the joint will move, but we don't know how to move it—this is a software problem. Both of these situations create imbalances in other places of the body. Stretching, yoga, dynamic warm-ups, and foam rolling are all quite different in how they act, and thus may not be the exact fix you need. To find the right answer for your individual movement problems, you need to understand what is limiting your mobility. From there, you can work toward safe, stable movement for your run.

MOBILITY IS NOT FLEXIBILITY

Flexibility is passive. You can pick up your shoe, and flex the toe box of the shoe back and forth. It can be moved, but the shoe can't flex the toe box by itself. Mobility is active. You can actively move your own toes up and down. While it may seem like semantics, this difference is critical in how we fix blocks in a runner's range of motion. And it's the key to helping Cole, Sam, and Jack squat correctly. There are several reasons why a runner may lack mobility.

In Eva's case, the ankle wasn't moving. After a 30-second stretch, the movement improved. Here's why: You've got a sensation in your body called proprioception. It's the ability to feel the positions of your joints, which is a sensory skill. This is why you can close your eyes and know whether your hand is open or clenched. Some of this sensation comes from "wires" in the joint surface and its surrounding tissue, and some comes from circuits within the muscle. These muscular circuits have names that sound important—the Golgi tendon organ and muscle spindle. These circuits are stimulated by load inside the muscle. If the strain inside the muscle gets too high, one of them turns on to tell the muscles to chill out and relax so it won't pull too hard and tear. The other does the opposite and tells the muscle "uh-oh, pull harder right now or we are going to be in trouble!" and stimulates a stronger contraction. They work together in a feedback loop to keep muscles working together to keep you safe and your movement precise.

After sitting in class all day Eva simply needed some extra time to warm up—not unlike your car engine on a cold day. Dynamic warm-ups have gained popularity in recent years, and with good reason. Some light movement, such as leg swings, hops, and other stuff we'll get to later, effectively prepares your nervous system to move smoother. From hours of inactivity Eva's Golgi tendons and muscle tendons were unstimulated, so they held the muscles around her ankle tight during the initial squats. The calf stretch lengthened the calf muscles—it doesn't take much to stimulate these two protective circuits. The circuits have a powwow and agree to stand down and allow Eva to move her ankle. This is dynamic warm-up in action. It's not stretching (even though it's called a calf stretch) and it's not increasing blood flow to the muscle. Rather it resets the muscle to allow you to move smoothly. But how do we know Eva improved based on her warm-up, and not something else? Actually, it's really the only plausible explanation, because a 30-second "stretch" isn't a big enough dose to cause a physical elongation of any structures around the ankle. Think of this as improving Eva's software.

PROPRIOCEPTIVE AWARENESS

MOBILITY SOFTWARE PROBLEMS

You don't look at your feet when you run. Instead you feel the position of your body. You are running down the road and you stumble on a rock. You don't have to look down to confirm the reality that your ankle rolled out—you can feel it. In that split second, something needs to happen or you are going to sprain your ankle. There is where the cross talk between your

structure, muscles, and brain, which we learned about in Chapter 1, factors in. Special nerves inside the ligaments relay a sensory phenomenon that helps us feel where our joints are; this is proprioception. This sensory input guides the way we move in real time and is relayed much faster than sight, smell, sound, or touch. The special nerves override the normal reflexive gait signals that are telling your body to push off and instead fire off a muscle sequence to quickly steer the inside of your foot safely back in line—and the ligaments outside of your ankle are forever grateful.

But you may not be a normal, healthy runner. Let's say that you are someone who sprains and rolls your ankles a lot. With every sprain, you are tearing the ligaments that surround the joint. The good news is that the ligament heals back to about 98 percent of its original strength to restore mechanical stability to the joint. But there's some bad news, too. Those proprioceptive nerves that run inside the ligament are torn for good. And it's permanent. With less sensory input coming into your brain to make the micro-corrections that keep your joints safe, your ankle control becomes sloppy.

When you feel wrong, you move wrong. The vast majority of ankle sprains—90 percent—occur when people roll out to the outside of the foot. If you are someone who rolls your ankles a lot, it seems that you would want to avoid walking and running with the ankle biased toward an outward roll. Ironically, a chronic ankle sprainer keeps the ankle rolled out all of the time, even when the foot is off the ground and swinging through the air, because they can't feel it.

However, it's not all bad news. Luckily, the body is a little redundant in how it handles inputs. With those nerves in the ligaments torn, there's another path to be wired. You can train the body to be more sensitive to the input it gets from the Golgi tendon and muscle spindle circuits inside the muscle and improve your feel of your ankle position.

better feel of your joint position = safer joint movement

It's not just about ankle sprains. Proprioception problems affect other parts of the body in the same way. Do you know what the biggest risk factor is for an ACL tear? It's not weakness, or genetics, or a dietary restriction. It's a prior ACL tear. You tear your ACL the first time because the way you moved your body was so sloppy that you broke your parts. You failed the "safe movement test." While you can surgically repair your ACL and make the knee more structurally stable, the research world classifies you as an athlete with "bad movement awareness." Because you couldn't move with precision the first time, research shows you aren't to be trusted in the future. In fact, you have a 20–50 times higher risk of tearing an ACL in the same knee or the opposite knee as compared to normal, healthy folks. But remember, these are just odds. Odds that people earn because they don't move well. Don't let yourself become a statistic. Just as putting a jet engine on a paper airplane won't make your plane fly farther, building strength on top of poor awareness isn't the answer. Learn how to own the movement for better, safer, and more efficient control of your body.

MOBILITY HARDWARE PROBLEMS

In contrast to Eva's software issue, Cole, Sam, and Jack aren't moving because something is wrong with their hardware. We ask each of them why they can't squat, and we get three different answers. Cole says he feel stiffness in front of his ankle. Sam says he feels tight in the back of his calf and Achilles. Jack says he is starting to get a little bit more motion with each rep, but his calves feel incredibly tight. We have three distinct hardware problems to address.

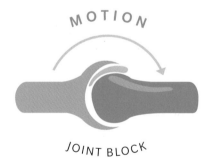

MOTION

JOINT BLOCK

Getting unstuck

Normally doors open and close. If you shove a doorstop under the door, it no longer swings freely, but it can still swing back the opposite way. Although joints are a little more complex than hinges, this is a great way to think about motion inside the joint. When joints move, they roll and glide on each other. We want to see Cole keep his foot flat on the ground so his shin can roll forward, but someone has stuck a doorstop in the front of his ankle. When the restriction you feel is on the side of the joint that is *shortening* it's a sign that the joint needs to improve the way it rolls and glides. Stretching won't work and typically causes more stiffness and pain. This is a good time to call your trusted physical therapist for some manual therapy work. In the chapters that follow, you will also find some DIY fixes to address problems with various body parts.

Lengthening tissue

Sam has problems on the opposite side of the ankle. He can't get his shin to roll forward because the parts on the backside of the joint (the calf muscles and Achilles) are too short to allow the motion. It's like when you went to Disney World as a kid and the sign in front of Space Mountain said "you must be this tall for this ride," and well, you just weren't tall enough. If the soft tissue length on the back of the joint is too short to allow the joints to roll and glide, it's time to stretch. When we stretch we are physically lengthening the tissue, tearing and ripping your muscle. It doesn't sound like such a great thing to do, does it? This is why stretching for stretching's sake doesn't make sense. If something is too short, then lengthen it. Otherwise stretching doesn't help anything, and in some situations it has been shown to impair performance. If you are a runner with a part that's too short, it takes time to physically lengthen your body parts. A 30-second stretch isn't enough to change tissue length. The research shows it takes about 3 minutes, 4–5 days a week, for about 10 weeks, to stretch a body part—i.e., to physically lengthen the tissue. If you need to stretch, it should always be done after your workout. We'll use the word "stretch" only in reference to long-hold static stretches. And yes, we'll look at some important stretches in Chapter 5.

Mobilizing tissue

It's time to figure out what is going on with Jack. He tells us that three days ago, he decided to run with his dad, Paul. While it was great bonding time, Paul is in peak shape and he took Jack on a hard 12-mile run in the mountains. Jack's calves are just shredded from running too many steep inclines. Hard running breaks down the body—and then it heals. One key variable in this breakdown and healing process has to do with the integrity and mobility of your fascia, a spiderweb-like layer of connective tissue covering layers of muscle, individual muscles, and even continuous around individual muscle fibers. Muscles contract and lengthen, but fascia doesn't move on its own. If everything is working well, fascia allows the muscle and tendon layers within it to slide and glide freely. But too much training volume can send the body into overdrive, causing the layers of tissue within the fascia to be stiff.

This brings us to a crossroads on how this stiffness materializes, and what we can do about it. These days there are a lot of claims made about fascia. Some people talk about it like voodoo. I teach gross anatomy and can tell you that fascia is very much real. However, the current understanding of fascia has not been able to identify if these restrictions are mechanical or neurologic. Let's explore both of the current hypotheses with respect to fascial restrictions:

- **Mechanical restrictions:** This camp thinks the fascia literally holds muscle fibers in a lockdown, limiting your motion and strength output. To visualize this theory, imagine putting on a pair of your snuggest running tights. Sticking your foot in and

TABLE 3.1 **Guidelines for Improving Your Mobility**

Problem	Solution	Takeaway
If your joint feels tight	Do a dynamic warm-up to improve proprioception prior to workout.	All athletes benefit from some type of dynamic warm-up to prepare to move well before a workout.
If your joint feels stuck	Do manual therapy to improve roll and glide of the joint prior to workout—1–2 minutes depending on body part.	If a joint feels stuck or is binding inside the joint, use a targeted approach to improve the roll and glide inside the joint. Stretching won't help, and likely will irritate the joint.
If you lack flexibility on the backside of your joint	Do post-workout stretching to lengthen your tissue—3 minutes done 5 days a week for 10 weeks.	If your tissue isn't long enough, stretch it. Otherwise, don't.
If the connective tissue around your joint feels stiff and bound down	Do tissue mobility work for 2 minutes per body part done before or after workout.	All runners accumulate soft tissue damage from high intensity and volume at various times of the season. Use a foam roller to target whatever feels stiff.

yanking them up as hard as you can would likely strain and tear the fabric. Instead, you have to use your hands to work them up and over the contours of your leg. Likewise, trying to stretch the fascial restrictions would shift those tightly bound stress points into longer, less tightly bound stress points. This camp proffers that the tissue mobilization "breaks up scar tissue." Now, the collagen fibers that make up fascia are 10 times stronger than steel. No offense, but I doubt your hands are strong enough to break steel fibers.

- **Neurologic restrictions:** These folks believe that the physical integrity of the fascia is fine, but for some reason, your nervous system is creating some type of guarding in the relationship of the fascia layers and muscle fibers. They claim that the act of compression and mobilization gives the nervous system input to downregulate (stand down!) and let things slide and glide again.

So, we aren't quite sure what's happening here. The approach of compressing the tissue with a foam roller, lacrosse ball, or your hands (or a masseuse's, if you are lucky!) and moving the tissue back and forth just may do something to improve the slide and glide of those tissue layers so you can run healthily. All we are doing is applying pressure and compression, and it does work—we just aren't sure why. But Jack just wants to feel better. And after a few minutes of rolling his calf on the foam roller, he suddenly feels great.

We'll highlight a few key tissue mobility moves in later chapters, but honestly, this is a problem you can solve pretty easily. If you are an endurance athlete, your body will go into hyper-repair mode at various times in the season. It's up to you to ensure you keep your tissues supple for running. It's worth your time to spend a few minutes each week rolling your thighs, shins, feet, or whatever feels stiff. Self-evaluation has its merits, and it's a good idea to put out smaller fires before they turn into forest fires.

So that makes four different runners. None of them moved correctly, but for completely different reasons. The same treatment doesn't work for everybody because not everyone has the same problem. Now, a few caveats. One person might actually need more than one of these interventions. If Cole's ankle joint has been mechanically blocked for years, it makes sense that the soft tissues in the backside of the joint would have adapted to not moving, and shortened over time. So if Cole does the ankle belt mobility exercise (p. 56) and is suddenly moving well, then great. But after we free up the joint glide problem, we might find that moving the shin forward now produces a super tight stretch in back of the joint. This means the joint block is cleared, but we now need to lengthen the muscles on the backside of the joint that have shortened up.

STABILITY IS CONTROLLED MOVEMENT

We can get runners unstuck, but that's just half of the job. Moving without control also creates instability and injury. Try to fire a cannon from a canoe, and your wobbly canoe will sink instantly. All that force requires something to help to keep it under control. If we were looking to stabilize a canoe we could add an outrigger on each side. But this doesn't help you as a runner—you have to build support within the system. Running throws huge loads at you whether you are ready for them or not. The only person capable of controlling those forces is you. If you can't control your body, you'll likely wind up like the 80 percent of runners who get hurt by running. Building control of your body can change you from a statistic into a runner.

Remember that mobility is *active*. If a runner frees up a joint, the runner needs to learn how to use this new motion, refining the micro-movement inside the joint. This comes with more proprioception training to help the body feel where it is. This sense of movement is relayed through the body to help us make a plan to move better. And this is the key difference between flexibility (passive movement) and mobility (active movement). Good mobility means the sloppy stuff is gone, and you are able to stabilize 100 percent of the movement of the joint.

When we talk about stabilizing a movement, we are not referring to static stability, as in holding an isometric plank. The body is dynamic and always moving when we run, so our stability needs to be dynamic as well. This is why most of the stability exercises in this book are dynamic. After all, our end goal is not to impress our friends with a 4-minute plank, but to improve mobility while running.

Stability impacts elasticity.

Dynamic control needs to be built in all three planes of running—vertical, side-to-side,

SAFE

NOT SAFE!

FIGURE 3.1 Move Safely
Stability keeps the joint position under control. Without proper stability, joints shift, movements become sloppy, and overload and injury can occur.

and forward-backward. If the muscles that keep the joint balanced aren't showing up, don't expect the movement to be balanced. We spend so much time running in the forward plane of motion that we develop relative imbalances in the muscles that steer our parts straight. We lose control and we lose precision in our movement.

huge forces + unstable levers = problems

Under optimal conditions, roughly half of the work required to propel you forward comes from storage and release of energy in the big rubber bands we call tendons. And when you are throwing this elasticity around, those tendons would like to have a solid foundation on which to attach. When you lack stability, tendons don't work as well as they should. This means your muscles have to work harder to make up the difference. Building better stability around your joints helps in transferring energy across the joints and improves economy.

By improving muscular control around the joints, we can decrease the compressive and shear load within your joints. Sloppy control around the joint creates instability and shear, which leads to premature wear and tear. Your muscles can rest and recover, but joint stress has bigger repercussions for your long-term health.

When you move with precision, you own the movement. And if you own the movement, you own your running form. Your reflexes are only as good as you allow them to be, so rather than run with a second-rate Plan B movement

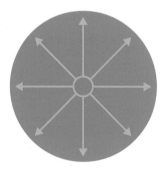 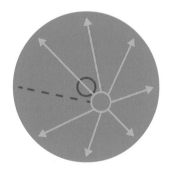

PLUGGED IN = BALANCE   **INHIBITED = IMBALANCE**

FIGURE 3.2 **Joint Balance versus Imbalance**
To move with precision, the muscles around the joint show up to balance out the stress across the joint. If all the muscles are plugged in, then the joint can move freely around its axis. However, if a muscle is inhibited (unplugged), the uniform tension the muscles create around the joint collapses. The axis changes, the joint is unstable, and joint health suffers.

pattern, let's begin fixing the underlying problems in the way you move. It's an easy two-step plan:

Step 1: Improve your joint roll and glide, tissue length, or fascial mobility to restore normal motion at the joint.

Step 2: Get connected to your body to build stability within the motion.

If It's Too Hard, You Won't Achieve Motor Learning

We talk about "balance training" all the time, but really you can't train balance. Balance is a broad term. However, there are key skills that you can build to improve your balance. As we saw in Chapter 1, better movement relies on your joints being integrated in the system so they can feel how to respond and tell your muscles to do something. For the vast majority of people with balance and stability issues, the problem is not that they are weak. Strength is the output—the thing we do. We need to sense, feel, and apply that information from our bodies to make a decision on how to balance (as shown in Figure 1.3). In other words, it's the sensory *input* that is the problem.

To train balance we need to improve how your body deals with the input signals that improve your balance. Everyone is different and starts out at a different place in the continuum. We've got runners Allie and Molly looking to improve their balance. Both of them decide to do 20 reps of the Tippy Twist exercise (which will be explained in Chapter 6), but they are not doing the reps in the same way. Allie has her arms outstretched like an airplane. She's using her arms as a counterbalance and flailing uncontrollably just hoping to not fall over. On the flipside, Molly is able to keep her hands on her hips and execute each rep as a smooth, fluid movement. She may not be able to twist her hips all the way in and out as she's still learning the exercise (just like Allie), but she's moving with control.

Here's where we need to use our brains and consider the context for each runner. When we look to build the skills of sensory input, we need to challenge—not overwhelm—the nervous system. This exercise is clearly meeting Molly where she is. She can maintain full foot contact, and she's doing a great job of hinging at the hip and twisting at the hip. And over the course of the next four sessions, we can expect the amount of twist in her hip to increase. Her nervous system is receiving an appropriate challenge and progressing.

Conversely, the same exercise is currently too advanced for Allie's nervous system. After four sessions it's unlikely that she will have made adequate progress—her movement will still be wobbly and unstable, causing her to use her arms for balance on each rep. The science of motor learning allows us to use constraints as a key method to train the brain. We have Allie place just one finger on a chair in front of her as she does the same exact exercise. This simple modification gives her brain an external reference point, and it's so helpful that she is now able to move with control through each rep. Her nervous system is no longer overwhelmed.

This means Allie can focus on the sensory info in her feet and hip, and over the course of the next few sessions, she's more likely to achieve plasticity and improve the quality and control of sensory input. And after just a few more sessions, she will probably be ready to remove that finger from the chair and place her hand back on her hip. Given time and the right starting place, Allie can move just as smoothly as Molly.

Using a finger, or even a hand as a reference point, reducing range of motion, or even intentionally blocking range of motion are all strategies to meet you where you are so you can progress. Throughout the exercises in this book, we'll highlight modifications to ensure you get the most motor learning out of the time you are investing. We always want the needle moving forward!

Scale your stability training to start from where you are and you will progress faster.

4

Your Body Drives Your Form

What does good form look like? Well, it looks like a lot of different things. Because people by nature are quite different, you aren't going to run exactly like your training partner or the person lined up next to you at the starting line, and quite honestly, you shouldn't. They aren't you! Some runners are tall. Some are short. Some have long thighs and short calves. Others have short thighs and long calves. Wide hips. Narrow hips. High-arch feet. Flat feet. There are people built like The Rock. And people built like an Olsen twin. We can't possibly expect everyone to land with the exact same knee angle or elbow angle or foot-strike position. Different is the norm in people, and different is the norm in form.

Even though we don't have a one-size-fits-all running formula, we do have some basic goals for good running form. Your running form should be 1) as economical as possible at a given speed, 2) as stress-free as possible, and 3) as symmetrical as possible. Let's dig a bit deeper.

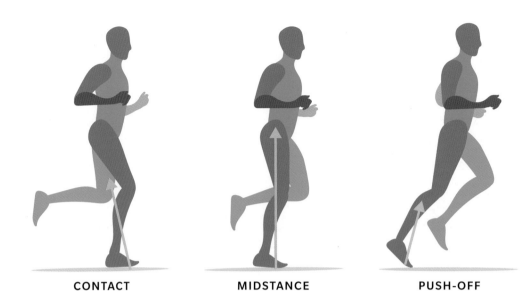

CONTACT   MIDSTANCE   PUSH-OFF

FIGURE 4.1 Running Economy
At contact, the ground reaction force puts you into an energy storage phase. At midstance, this force is aligned with the body (there is no braking or drive), which demands maximal stability. At push-off, this stored elastic energy is released to drive forward.

GOAL 1: RUNNING ECONOMY

This is defined as the energy required to run a certain speed. It's a little like fuel efficiency in a car: A vehicle with better gas mileage, measured in miles per gallon (mpg) can go farther on the same amount of fuel than a car with lower mpg. If you improve your running economy, you can run faster at the same perceived effort and lower energy expenditure.

Ideally, about half the work required to run comes from active muscle contraction, and the other half comes from stored elasticity in the tendon. Think about a slingshot—you can't fire the rock unless you cock it back first. From foot contact until midstance (when the foot is directly under the body), energy is stored in the tendons. From midstance until push-off, we fire the rock. This stored energy is released to help drive us forward. Improving running economy is all about capitalizing on elastic recoil to save our muscles. There are quite a few things that can boost your running economy, but form stands out. Specifically posture alignment and where your foot contacts the ground in relation to your body affect the use of your elasticity. As a general rule, you want to maintain a neutral spine position and strike the ground as close to your body as you can for a given pace.

GOAL 2: LOW-STRESS RUNNING

The stress-per-stride that your body endures when running is driven by two main factors. And, interestingly, it's these two factors that are responsible for essentially all of the sport's overuse injuries.

Overstriding

Runners who land with their foot too far in front of their body, called overstriding, are often overwhelmed by the loading rate. Why? The 250 percent body weight load they must deal with on each stride ramps up too quickly. If they keep doing this for miles on end, their bodies break. And keep on breaking. Let's consider how this works with a common overuse injury. Stress fractures in the front of the shin (tibia) are typically a result of two distinct issues. In terms of gait, the runner is overstriding, throwing load at the body too quickly. And on top of that, the runner typically has a stiff foot that doesn't do a good job at absorbing shock. Consequently, all that excess load goes right up into the shin. Put these problems together and you've got a perfect recipe for overload—and a stress fracture.

To help this runner, we would need to first get his foot working so it can do its job of dissipating the stress with less trauma channeled up to the shin. Then we'd work to achieve foot contact closer to the body. For those of you who like numbers: Let's say Keith is running with a loading rate of 7,500 Newtons/second (N/s) and we improve his gait to achieve a number in the range of 5,000 N/s. This means he has roughly 33 percent less tissue strain on his body with every stride for all his weekly mileage. Win. Fixing the foot and bringing the point of contact closer to the body require strategies revealed in Chapter 11.

We All Land in Front of Center

It's commonly said that you should "land with your foot under your center of mass," but unless you are accelerating, it is physically impossible to land with your foot directly under your center of mass. I can bring to my lab any form guru or any runner from any school of running bias and demonstrate that at steady-state speed every single runner on planet Earth contacts in front of his or her center of mass. It is true that contacting too far out in front of you, or overstriding, is bad for a number of reasons—namely that it increases the mechanical stress of running and hurts economy. However, landing slightly in front of your center of mass is good because it allows us to store energy in the tendons, thereby reducing the force you need to generate with your muscles. Do you want to know what it's like to run without the storage and release of energy in the tendons? Try sprinting. When you sprint, the time on the ground is so short that the elasticity can't be absorbed and then rebound. This is why you need to take a break after sprinting for 100 meters. Elasticity is the reason you can run all day at an easy pace.

Landing on the Forefoot

There is a contingent still pushing the message that runners must land on the forefoot. I'll share with you some reconnaissance on that topic. Years ago, I was invited to a barefoot running event in New York City. This was a passionate group of runners who considered running shoes to be an unnecessary evil. They preached that unless you were running on your forefoot, you were running wrong. A friend of mine planted a video camera in the bushes and filmed these runners as they went by. Among this group of highly passionate runners, over half of them were not landing on the forefoot. Most of them were closer to midfoot, and a surprising number of runners were landing on the heel.

Footstrike is worth talking about. However, it's one tree in a big forest. Making contact on the forefoot can greatly decrease loading rate, but it costs extra energy to run this way. Additionally, research has shown that most runners will change their footstrike as they fatigue, and pace and running surface play a big role here as well. And a forefoot strike has not been shown to be more efficient. Consequently, I typically don't cue a foot landing position. It's best to just let your footstrike style happen naturally. Where the foot contacts in relation to your body is much more important than where you make contact on your foot. Ain't nothin' wrong with a heel strike!

TABLE 4.1 Effects of Footstrike and Foot Placement

	Stress	Economy
If you overstride, landing on your heel	High stress because the foot makes contact too far in front of the body.	Extra work is required to lift the body up and down more, overloading the muscles on the front side of the legs.
If you run with a pendulum-like stride	Low stress, ideal load.	Optimal elastic recoil makes for more efficient running.
If you overstride, landing on your forefoot	Low stress because the ankle muscles are absorbing the load.	Ankle muscles work overtime to maintain forefoot position. Excessive acceleration and deceleration with each stride compromise efficiency.

Instability

Runners must stabilize the forces acting on them in all three planes of motion. If they can't control their position, things get wobbly. It's normal to have some side-to-side wobble, and it's a part of the normal shock-absorption strategy of a healthy gait. However, when people can't stabilize their parts, we see their entire body start to wobble too much and with too much variability. Let's take another look at a stress fracture developing in the shin. However, this time there's a completely different reason for this diagnosis—the runner's foot coordination is off. Since muscles inside the foot aren't firing, the muscle that decelerates the foot on the shin is forced to work much harder than it needs to. The overworked muscle yanks on the shin bone and eventually cracks the outer wall of the bone right off. In this situation, the primary goal is to improve the coordination and control of muscles inside the foot so the body can maintain its alignment and position when running. Next, we need to look around the rest of the body to see if we can identify any red flags that indicate the runner is unstable and making the body work too hard. (You will find out how to spot these in later chapters.) High body stress, either due to lack of shock absorption or instability, can cause tissues to be overloaded. The goal in both of these situations is to ensure that we improve form to make running less stressful, and to get your body parts to work together properly to control your movement and reduce the stress per stride.

GOAL 3: SYMMETRY

Some people are left-handed, and some people are right-handed. You have better fine motor skill on one hand to write and draw. No problem here. And those of you who played soccer likely noticed that your goal shots and passes were more accurate when you kicked with your right foot. Again, when dealing with fine motor accuracy in this situation, an asymmetry is no problem. But gross motor tasks like running require both legs to show up equally. No one wants to run with a limp. If you sprained your ankle three days ago and can barely walk, it wouldn't be smart to meet your friends for an easy 8-miler. If you can't move symmetrically, you won't run symmetrically. And asymmetry eventually comes back to haunt you.

WHEN FORM SWINGS OUT OF BALANCE

Right from the start we made it clear that these three aspects of running form occur under "ideal conditions." To understand what this looks like, let's envision a grandfather clock. It's normal to have a slight arch in your low back, and we want to preserve that normal curve in a neutral spine posture. The upright grandfather clock echoes the idea that the upper body is generally upright. The pendulum swings freely from side to side, just as the legs swing from front to back for an efficient and low-stress stride. Let's see what happens when we change the clock.

If we tilt the clock forward or backward it will affect the swing of the pendulum. In the same way, running with poor posture shifts where your foot is in relation to your body mass. Interestingly, either excessive low back arch or leaning too far forward both increase the distance from foot contact in front of the body mass, which impairs economy and increases the stress-per-stride. The take-home here is that your upper body posture should be mostly upright with a slight forward lean.

Sometimes it's the swing of the pendulum that creates issues. Running a certain pace requires you to have a certain stride length, requiring your leg to swing through an arc below your body. If you show up with a stiff hip that won't let you extend your leg behind you, the dynamics of the pendulum will shift. While the distance the leg must swing beneath the body must stay the same, the swing shifts to extend farther in front, and less in back. This imbalance changes the dynamics of the slingshot by curtailing your elastic recoil. You store

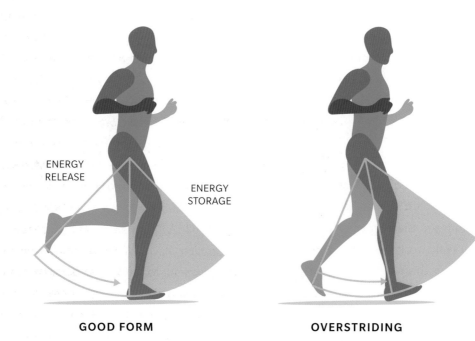

ENERGY RELEASE

ENERGY STORAGE

GOOD FORM

OVERSTRIDING

FIGURE 4.2 **Pendulum Shift**

With good form, you encounter minimal stress-per-stride and optimal economy. When you make contact too far in front of the body, or overstride, it requires that you lift the body up and down more, overloading the muscles on the front side of the legs and increasing the stress-per-stride. A symmetric pendulum builds a successful stride.

more energy in the slingshot, but blocks in your body prevent it from being released. Elastic recoil is compromised, muscle work goes up, and running economy tanks. Additionally, the foot contacting out in front increases the stress on your body due to the higher loading rate. And now imagine that you've got two pendulums—two legs—swinging opposite each other. They've got to be in sync or else things will end up out of balance. That's symmetry at work.

CADENCE

The idea that a higher cadence can help you run better has been a hot topic for some time. The reality is that most runners do overstride. When runners increase their cadence, they have less time to swing the lead leg as far forward as they typically do. Remember that any form change that enables the foot to land closer to the body is a great strategy to reduce your stress-per-stride and improve economy. It is actually more metabolically efficient to take more smaller steps than it is to take fewer longer steps at a given pace, but again, this is under ideal conditions.

But what feels good at one pace may not feel the best at all paces. When running easy, your leg turnover doesn't need to be as high to maintain speed. It's normal to run with a slightly slower turnover since you aren't covering as much distance per time. Bigger issues occur when we talk about running faster paces. Some runners note that it feels hard to run faster with a higher turnover, which they might describe as being unable to stride out. This is a big clue. To run a specific speed requires a certain turnover and stride length. The cadence cue typically helps runners shorten their stride up front, but they need to open up the swing of their pendulum out the back to increase their stride length, and some runners just don't know how to move this way. Their preferred method of increasing speed is to elongate their stride from the front. Running economy typically gets worse as these runners pick up speed. This is not a cadence problem, but rather a body awareness problem that can be improved with training.

YOUR BODY DRIVES YOUR FORM

Father Time has taught us a good lesson here. Chances are that you would like to craft a running stride that lowers the stress per stride and boosts your performance. And you've likely picked up on my not-so-subtle argument that your own body is the single biggest obstacle standing in the way of achieving your peak running form.

Improving Cadence

Before you set out to increase your cadence, there are a few important points you'll want to keep in mind. First, running with your existing cadence is reflexive. Your brain has wired and trained your body to use that gait pattern. Modifying this pattern requires your brain to do a huge amount of work to override your reflexive gait. If you force too high of a turnover the result will be an oddly short and choppy run as your brain overthinks your turnover. While this strategy can reduce the stress to your joints, it costs significantly more energy to run this way. Through training it is possible to improve your gait, but it should be done gradually.

This brings us to the mythical optimal cadence. Many tout the idea of 180 steps a minute as the gold standard. Some research does support 180 as an average optimal value, but not everyone's average. So it serves as a nice reference point, but it's not absolute. Your optimal cadence depends on your muscle fiber type, limb length, tendon density, terrain, and speed. World records have been achieved at cadences between 172 and 212 steps per minute. I wouldn't stress about where you fall in this range or how close your cadence is to 180. Then who should make efforts to adjust their cadence? If your cadence is less than 170 at a moderate pace, it is worth your time to improve it a bit. Rather than struggle to hit 180, try to increase it by 5–10 percent at a time. Research has shown that this smaller percentage increase provides benefits to your joints without compromising economy. Likewise, it's beneficial to monitor your cadence over longer runs. It's normal to have some variation of approximately 5 percent during a run at a given pace. If your cadence drops from 176 to 160 toward the end of your weekly long run, it's a sign that your form is vastly different when fatigued.

Log your cadence in both runs and races in your training journal for a month, and look for patterns in both. If your racing cadence is always higher than your training cadence, you should start to practice what you preach on race day and ensure your nervous system can maintain higher cadence runs during the week. Likewise, if you are one of the runners we mentioned above who just can't stride out at race pace with a lower racing cadence, it's time to unlock your form to ensure you can get the pendulum to swing out behind you at speed. Be mindful of your cadence, but don't be a slave to it.

Training places stress on your body. The body is actually quite good at adapting to body stress, as long as increases in volume and intensity are progressive. But training with your Plan B running form is far from your individual optimal gait. And training with a poorly prepared body means you'll never be able to improve your form. If you can't maintain posture and achieve a pendulum-like leg swing, you'll never be able to hit your best running form. You'll be stuck in a Plan B running gait. Deliberate practice of specific skills will unlock your body and transform your stride from a Plan B workaround to a Plan A optimal stride. Get your body out of the way and let your new muscle memory take over.

At this point, we have identified some specific skills that may be a roadblock to your running. Now it's time to divide and conquer. When you bring these skills to each and every workout and race, you are able to run your best. The Running Rewired program will focus on precision movement and durability in:

1. Postural control
2. Rotational stability
3. Triple Extension
4. Individual skeletal alignment
5. Building Better Parts

In the chapters that follow we are going to make the case for each of these skills and provide fixes to ensure that you can move with precision. Some problems in the way we move are due to mobility blocks, some are due to muscles not controlling our body well enough for proper stability, and some are due to bad habits and muscle memory. We'll break this down together. In some cases there will be special tests and corrections for mobility blocks. If you have mobility issues, I'm going to ask you to make time to address them because they won't fix themselves. Every few weeks or months, run yourself through the test again and see if you still need some help. If so, keep going with the adjustments. If you pass with flying colors, you can move on because our workout plan will build on your new and improved movement once you've unblocked your body.

In each section, we will introduce new movements that apply to the concept presented. After you read each chapter, practice each movement. Deliberate practice is eye-opening, and it may push you out of your comfort zone, but that's the state in which you learn muscle memory best. If you want to change your body, you need to change what you are doing on a consistent basis. So try out each move as introduced. In the workout section, you'll see I've selectively placed these movements into these workouts to help you improve your skill, precision, and athleticism for better running.

5

Don't Break Your Pivot Point

Several years ago, I worked with a collegiate runner who was struggling with low back pain. College kids are healthy and spry—they aren't supposed to have low back pain. In the clinic, this runner could find and demonstrate perfect, pain-free spine positioning, but while running, he was in pain. So I went to the track and watched a few of his workouts. I noticed that he ran in the "back seat"—his back had an exaggerated arch that created a stress point in his low back. This stress worsened as his speed increased. Remember that 250 percent body weight load that runners support with every step? Well, with this runner, that load was magnified in his lower back. No matter how strong this athlete's core became, his poor back position caused overload. The more he ran, the more he continued to irritate the tissues at fault, and he never had a chance to actually get better.

But posture is not easily changed. Posture reflects your core strength, your mobility, and your habits. Certain positions feel normal and others feel forced, odd, incorrect. Instead of giving this runner more core work to do, we had to change his perception through practice.

So we made a deal. He was allowed to run as much as he wanted, and as fast as he wanted in training, as long as he maintained a healthy spine position while running. When he ran with good posture, he ran like the wind. When his form fell apart—whether from fatigue or his mind drifting off—his workout was over. Period. There is no sense in practicing and reinforcing bad habits.

Later that season he ran in the national championships in the 800. The start gun fired, and eight guys ran their hearts out in a display of amazing fitness. Just 200 meters from the finish, everybody got tired. As if on cue, five of the eight runners fell into the back seat. Instantly, they were out of view of the TV camera and off-screen. The extra energy it takes to run with poor posture took them out of the race. The three guys who maintained proper postural alignment crossed the line 1, 2, and 3. And our athlete won in what was one of the most amazing races I've ever seen. But that win isn't the point of my story.

It's this: Running with poor posture will cost you energy. In Chapter 1 we asked, "What does it take to get from here to there?" Smart training should cover each and every aspect that you can improve, so that your running can improve. We know running is tiring and everyone gets fatigued. You need to ensure that your body is wired to maintain correct form under stress, because stress is your true nemesis. Why put yourself in a position to have to work harder to maintain speed in the last 200 meters of the NCAA national championship? Or your local 5K?

Some people think running posture is just a detail. But posture is not a detail—it's one of the most important aspects of running form. You know the new breed of super shoes everyone is freaking out about? They claim to improve your running economy by 2–4 percent. Step into my lab and I'll show you that postural control can improve your running economy by 1–8 percent, no shoes required! Good running posture keeps your body healthy and helps you beat the clock. Let's take a closer look at how posture affects the body and performance.

REDEFINING CORE STABILITY

Drink your favorite beverage, then set the empty can on the table. Without liquid or carbonation inside, the top and bottom are supported only by the cylinder itself. This construction provides a lot of strength, even when the can is empty. Place a 10-pound weight on top, and the can will support the load.

good position = good stability
poor position = instability

Now take this same can, dimple the side a bit, and put the same weight back on top. The can will crumple under the load.

When you run, you have to support around 250 percent of your body weight with each and every step for miles on end. If your can is crushed, you can't keep your parts in position. This creates two major problems:

1. You lose some coordination and your movements start to get sloppy.
2. You have to work harder to run.

Your brain is hardwired from an early age to put the body in a position of stability centrally (in the core) and to move distally (through the arms and legs). When that central link is blown, certain muscles unwire themselves from normal reflexive movement, others fire late, and you lose the ability to move with precision. When posture and alignment are compromised, the types of inhibition we discussed in Chapter 2 begin to get your attention. The stress isn't distributed around the entire wall of the can, but is focused at certain points which then become overstressed. Parts of your body that usually tolerate a given amount of strain as you run are now asked to tolerate even more stress, which sets you up for injury. Because good movement requires a fully functional system, you have to look past isolated parts to find the root of the problem. For example, a lot of runners do hip exercises without experiencing improvements in hip control or running form because the link between their hips and their core is faulty.

Finding Neutral in an Un-Neutral World

Think about how many minutes each week you spend . . .

☐ sitting in an office chair?
☐ standing in a slumped position?
☐ walking with a heavy load?
☐ walking in heels?
☐ hunched over your iPhone?
☐ running?

Most of us spend a significant amount of time reinforcing bad postural alignment. This starts early in life—think of kids carrying overloaded backpacks and spending hours slumped over their devices. We are creatures of habit. How many signals is your brain getting to imprint this position into the way you sit, stand, walk, squat? You spend more hours not running than you spend running. Practicing poor posture in daily life teaches us to move a certain way, and that's all we learn. This postural alignment becomes who we are. And then we put our running shoes on and expect to have perfect alignment for our 3-mile tempo run and our upcoming half-marathon. Finding and feeling posture awareness is key: If you can't stand right, you can't run right.

Poor postural alignment shifts where the foot contacts with respect to your body position, which cripples your propulsion and increases body stress. Whether you slump forward or lean backward, your foot will contact the ground too far in front of your body—the dreaded overstride. Do you really want to work harder than you need to at a given pace? I didn't think so.

What's crushing your can?

When dealing with a dimpled or crushed can, many athletes will add crunches and core work, thinking core strength will fix everything. Training your core is important, but unless your goal is posing on the bodybuilding stage, you shouldn't train your core in isolation. Let's look at how problems above or below the core can crush your can—even if you can hold a plank for 20 minutes.

You have two big ball-and-socket joints both below and above the core. Below the core, each hip should be able to swing freely from front to back without cranking your low back into an arch. Above the core, you should be able to reach your arm overhead without arching your low back. But once again, you can only move as efficiently as your body allows. Sitting and slumping for hours on end tightens the muscles around the front of the hips and pulls the shoulders forward. These mobility restrictions on top of the can (your shoulders) and below the can (your hips) will crumple your can from the top, or bottom, or both. And so you adapt.

NORMAL MOBILITY   LIMITED MOBILITY   LIMITED MOBILITY
                              ABOVE   BELOW

FIGURE 5.1 Don't Crush the Can
When the shoulders and hips can move freely, posture is kept in check. Motion blocks above or below the core force the back to move instead of the shoulders or hips. When this central pivot point in the core breaks down, so does your running form.

This crumpled position becomes the new normal as you stand, walk, and run. You might be strong enough to power through an exercise, but there's no sense in fighting your body every step of the way.

Unloading the top of the can

I have lost count of the number of runners I have seen with significant problems with posture, running mechanics, and even lower-body injuries that are driven by upper-body issues. As the tissues in the shoulders tighten, they pull the shoulder blades forward. And over time, they pull the mid back (the thoracic spine) forward with it. And the mid back and ribs get stiffer and stiffer. The front of the can starts to crumple—and your mom or coach tells you to stand up straight. But the mid back, ribs, and shoulders have become so tight, you can't fix the front of the can. Instead you arch your low back to compensate, which crumples the back of the can, which further complicates the inhibition problem. And this position creates breathing restrictions as well. Instead of your ribs expanding laterally and down to allow diaphragmatic breathing, you have to raise them up against gravity with chest breathing. In the worst-case scenario, runners can waste 10 percent of their energy breathing. That's energy that would be better spent driving the body forward.

To unload the can, we need to apply what we learned about mobility. The upper-body posture problems will require a combination of improving glide at the joints, lengthening the structures that are tight and bound down, and then building control of the new motion.

The back is made of bones called vertebrae. If each of those vertebrae attached to only one other bone, as they do in the neck and low back, we would have a fair amount of motion available to twist our head and lumbar spine. But the mid-back vertebrae anchor the ribs. And after you count the joints between the vertebrae, and the rib attachments above and below each vertebra, there are 12 different joints on each thoracic vertebra. So many joints around one bone imposes a lot of stiffness into the system. It's why you can't move your mid back as freely as the rest of your spine.

If you have excessive tightness in your mid back, it's a joint problem, not a flexibility problem. It's not possible to stretch your mid back, and you can't actively reverse the curve in your mid back either. In order to improve the motion on the shortened side of the joint we need to use some props.

Once we improve the joint glide of the vertebrae and ribs, we can use a traditional stretch to open the pec minor muscle in front of the chest that is pulling us forward. Because a slumped spine puts your pecs into a shortened position, you can't stretch the pecs in front until you open the stiffness in the back. Opening the spine gets you more length in the front of the chest so that stretching can be effective. If you have struggled with a stiff mid back, do the Travolta peanuts or the basketball mobility exercises 1–2 times every week or until you begin to feel the stiffness improving.

Once your chest is all set, we'll use a little trick to help drive your shoulder blades down and back to the place they should be, and reinforce this position with a simple band exercise. The overhead carry and the shoulder pack exercises (banded arm circles and banded pull-aparts) will play a role in the Running Rewired workouts that you will find after Chapter 11.

The good news is that this sequence isn't as complex as it may seem. In fact, this entire routine takes less than 10 minutes, and it is a powerful way to improve your posture. If you have posture issues, the full Posture Fix routine that follows will feel incredible. You'll be surprised to find out how much your posture really can improve. Do the work and straighten out the side—or sides—of your can.

BASKETBALL MOBILITY

- Sit on the floor with a basketball, soccer ball, or even a hard medicine ball behind you, feet on the floor and knees bent. Put your hands behind your head, elbows pointing forward, and lean back on the ball, positioning yourself so your mid back rests on the ball.

- Keep your head and elbows pointed toward your knees. Don't look up at the ceiling—you want the fulcrum of the ball to be at your mid back, not your neck.

- Spend 2–3 minutes rolling the ball up and down along your spine and laterally into the ribs to find spots that feel stiff. Rest on these spots, breathing in and out, and try doing small crunches. Think about relaxing and extending into the ball as you return to resting position— don't curl up into a tight crunch.

- Work from the shoulder blades down to the bottom of the rib cage. Do not go into the lower back.

TIPS

Spend a few breaths in each spot. After a few sessions, you'll know which areas need regular work.

The benefit comes with the exhale. Holding your breath stiffens the mid back, so relax into the movement and breathe so your ribs glide.

Note: If you have a history of osteoporosis, skip this exercise as it places a lot of pressure on a focal point in your back.

Lacrosse balls are used in physical therapy to improve mobility. Tightly tape together two lacrosse balls with athletic tape (or duct tape), wrapping the tape tightly in a figure-eight pattern. When you are finished, it will look like a peanut.

TRAVOLTA PEANUTS

■ Lie on your back with your knees bent and your feet flat on the floor. Place the peanut horizontally under your mid back at the bra line (or "bro line") and rest your head on the floor.

■ Hold small weights (2–3 lbs.) in each hand and reach them up to the ceiling. Relax and allow the weight to glide your shoulder blades back and open.

■ Reach one arm up overhead so the weight contacts the floor, and drop the opposite arm down along your side.

■ Do 10 reaches (5 reps on each side). Then move your body down approximately 1 inch so that the peanut moves up to hit the next vertebra in your mid back. Repeat the reps with your arms.

■ Continue until the peanut is a few inches below the bump at the base of your neck.

TIPS

Yes, this feels intense, but it works well. If you are chronically stiff, do this corrective exercise regularly.

The work happens as you exhale, so relax into the movement.

The small hand weights will help you relax, so for best results, don't skip them. (If you don't have light weights, cans of soup or beer will work just fine.)

Note: If you have a history of osteoporosis, skip this exercise as it places a lot of pressure in focal points on your back.

Step 2: Open the front of the chest

PEC MINOR STRETCH

- To stretch the left side: Lie on your stomach with your left arm out to the side at 90 degrees to your body, and walk it out laterally until all the slack is gone in the front of your chest. Gently bend your left elbow about 45 degrees.

- Place your right hand under your right shoulder and push so that the right side of your body twists off the floor.

- Bend your knees and hips up to 90 degrees on your right side and relax. You'll feel the stretch in the front of the left shoulder.

- Hold this position for 2–3 minutes. Switch sides.

TIPS

This position allows you to stretch the muscle and the nerve. If you feel numbness or tingling in your fingers, drop your elbow a bit closer to your waist. This modification will decrease the stretch you feel in the muscle a little, but more importantly, it will also unload the nerve. Nerves don't like to be stretched!

The floor supports your shoulder, which makes this a safe way to stretch the pec minor. The classic doorway or wall stretch can cause shoulder instability and should be avoided.

Step 3: Put your shoulder blades back where they belong

OVERHEAD CARRY

For this movement you'll need an Olympic bar (45 lbs.) or a lighter trainer bar (15–45 lbs.), both of which can be found at most gyms. At home you can use a broomstick or PVC pipe with a few ankle weights on each end. The key is to get the bar heavy enough that it pushes the shoulder blades down, but not so heavy that you strain to hold it up.

- Hold the bar with your hands about six inches wider than your shoulders, palms facing forward when overhead.

- Press the bar overhead until your elbows are locked straight. Focus on keeping your rib cage dropped down slightly in front to avoid arching your low back.

- Walk for at least 45 seconds. Do 3 sets.

TIPS

Keep your ribs low. When your arms move up, don't allow your chest to follow suit.

Let the weight of the bar push your shoulder blades back and down. Don't try and shrug it up any higher once overhead.

Relax your neck and focus on keeping your elbows locked and the weight will take care of the rest.

BANDED ARM CIRCLES

- Stand, feet shoulder-width apart, holding a TheraBand (or resistance band) in both hands about waist level with your palms facing forward. Widen your grip to place some tension on the band. Your hands should be positioned 10–12 inches wider than your shoulders.

- Keep your elbows locked as you reach overhead, then behind your body with the band, and then back to center.

- Do 20 reps of this movement, then go straight into the pull-aparts (p. 52).

PULL-APARTS

- Hold a TheraBand in your hands about waist high, arms straight and hands about shoulder-width apart. Keep your elbows locked and raise your arms until they are just below your shoulders.

- Pull the band ends in opposite directions until your arms are spread wide, then release to starting position.

- Do 20 reps.

Looking below the can

As you run, your legs should be able to swing in front and behind your body. I've never seen a distance runner who couldn't get their legs in front of their body while running. But the backside is another story. It's critical that your leg can swing freely behind you without exaggerating the arch in your low back. Let's test and tackle this now.

Hip Mobility Test

■ Kneel inside a doorway, with your mid back touching the doorframe. The thigh you are kneeling on should be vertical, and the shin of your opposite leg should also be vertical. In this position, you'll have a small gap between your low back and the doorframe.

■ Now, tuck your tailbone under so that the hollow between your low back and the doorframe disappears. To make this happen, imagine your pelvis as a bowl of cereal that you are trying to spill behind you. This movement is commonly referred to as pelvic tilt. Once you are in this position, what do you feel?

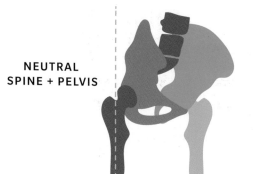

NEUTRAL SPINE + PELVIS

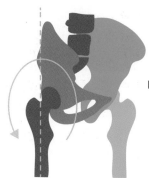

PELVIC TILT

If you feel a huge pull in front of the thigh		Incorporate the kneeling hip flexor stretch (p. 54) into your weekly maintenance work.
If you feel nothing or just a gentle lengthening		There is no need to do any static stretches in the hip flexors. The Running Rewired Workouts build in plenty of dynamic mobility movement to ensure you use the hip motion you do have.

KNEELING HIP FLEXOR STRETCH

- Kneel on a pad or pillow, making sure to keep the thigh of the leg you are kneeling on vertical.

- Tuck your pelvis under (see the posterior pelvic tilt instruction in the hip mobility test on p. 53). Hold this position for 3 minutes.

- To increase the stretch, position the foot of your kneeling leg out to the side a few inches (this will rotate your thigh inward) before moving into a posterior pelvic tilt.

Ankle Mobility Tests

- Take your shoes off and stand facing a wall. Place your big toe right at the base of the wall, and bend your ankle until your kneecap touches the wall.

- If your kneecap touches the wall without causing your heel to lift off of the floor, you have all the motion you need to run. (Test both sides.) Now we also need to ensure that you can nail your form in some of the squat workouts we'll do. Squatting requires a bit more ankle motion. Without it, you will cheat the motion in your spine.

- Mark a line on the floor about 5 centimeters from the wall. Now place your big toe on this line, and again try to touch your kneecap to the wall.

- If you make it without the heel coming up, you pass! If not, let's examine what is preventing full movement. Make sure to test both sides.

If you failed either test (toes at the wall or at 5 cm), do these exercises below to correct the problem.

If you feel tightness in front of the ankle	➤	Do the ankle belt mobility exercise, p. 56.
If you feel tightness in back of the ankle	➤	Do the burrito calf stretch, p. 57.
If you can hit the wall, but your calves are stiff	➤	Do the calf smash, p. 57.

THE POSTURE FIX

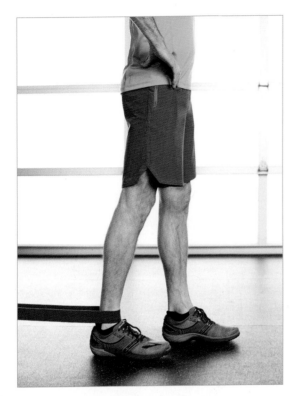 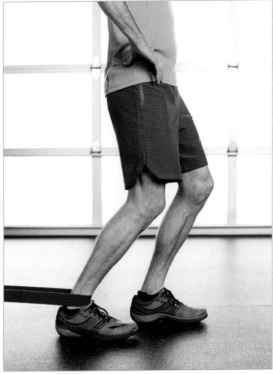

ANKLE BELT MOBILITY

- Position a belt around something sturdy and place one leg inside the loop. Turn so the attachment point is behind you and slide the belt down to your ankle.

- Step your foot forward to remove any slack in the belt. It should be tight just above the ankle joint in the front.

- Keep your foot fully flat on the ground and move your shin forward, as the belt glides the front of the ankle backward. Hold for 1 or 2 seconds, and relax.

- Do 20 reps and switch legs if both sides are tight.

BURRITO CALF STRETCH

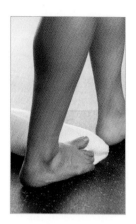

- Stand with your foot on top of a rolled towel so that your big toe is positioned on the "burrito roll" and your little toes drape off the side.

- Bend your knee forward while keeping your heel flat and square to the floor. Hold this stretch for 3 minutes. You will feel this across the back of the calf.

CALF SMASH

- Sit on the floor with a foam roller under one calf, and cross your opposite leg on top. Put your hands behind your butt and lift your weight onto your hands and calf.

- Roll your calf up and down on the roller and find spots that feel stiff. Flex and extend your ankle to better address tightness.

- Do this for 2 minutes a few days a week until your calf feels supple.

▷ NEW POSTURE, NEW RUNNING FORM

It's important to be able to find and feel your neutral spine. Once you know what it feels like to stand straight, you can replicate your best posture in standing, walking, doing these exercises, and even when running. Better posture helps your body work at its best in everything you do.

Remember, everyone has a curve in his or her neck, mid back, and low back. It helps with shock absorption. If paratroopers land with a straight spine, they run a very high risk of their backbones literally exploding on impact. Running with poor posture is not likely to blow up your back, but we can agree that running will feel better if the normal curvature of your spine can absorb some of the shock. Everyone has somewhat different anatomy, but we can figure out your specific posture alignment by feel.

Many runners (and trainers) think that an arched low back is bad, and so they try to

Posture Test

This test is easy: Stand up with your feet roughly shoulder width apart and relax into your normal posture. Go on and give it a try. Where is your weight? (Yes, you actually need to do this part!)

If your weight is at midfoot		Great! This is the best position for doing anything active. This is your neutral spine position.
If your weight is at rearfoot		Place one hand on your belly button, and one hand on your breastbone. Keeping the lower hand and the belly still, slightly drop the ribs down and forward until you feel the balance point shift away from your heels and to your midfoot. Make sure you are moving from the rib cage—not from the neck! Now maintain this trunk position and let your arms hang down by your sides. Rotate your hands so your palms point forward, which will help screw your shoulder blades down and along your back. Now, keep the shoulder blades back and relax your arms.
If your weight is at forefoot		You are likely leaning too far forward from the ankles, or leaning forward from the low back. Pull your hips back slightly with respect to your feet and see how you feel. If this brings your weight over your midfoot, great. If you are now on your heels, run through the rearfoot sequence above.

Once you find your neutral spine position, stand on one leg and then the other. Make a mental imprint of how this position feels and come back to it every day, on every run, until it's wired into your muscle memory.

correct their posture by drawing the belly up and in, which puts their tailbone in a tucked position. This doesn't work for two reasons.

First, it tasks important muscles with the wrong job. The deep spinal muscles stabilize the walls of your can. If you tuck your tailbone, you inadvertently end up using the muscles that flex the spine (your rectus abdominus, or six-pack)

to move the tailbone, which makes the walls unstable and ultimately crumples the can. Your six-pack is for show, not for go.

Making matters worse, a tucked tailbone affects your range of motion. Try to tuck your tailbone and then take a step. You will find that it's nearly impossible to move. Tucking under the tailbone uses nearly all of the available hip extension range you've got, and now you can't move your hip behind you. It doesn't work. It's important to feel that this doesn't work, so you can rule out this strategy once and for all. In a case where a runner has a prominent lumbar curve, our corrections happen above the pelvis.

The first time you do the posture test and correct into a midfoot weight bias, you may feel like you're fighting yourself. If that's the case, you likely have a mobility or stability block on the top or bottom of your can that is trying to pull you out of your ideal alignment. Before you do anything else, I strongly recommend that you fix any blocks. Do try to make changes, but if you've got a block, you have to fix the block as we outlined in the tests. You can only move as well as your body allows you to. As mobility improves and as you continue to progress through the exercises to rewire your movement, this will start to feel more normal.

Building a solid foundation will positively affect loads in your back, your balance, the stress your body sees, and ultimately your run times. Repetition of correct movement builds habit, and posture is a display window for your habits. The more you practice good posture when not running, the easier it will be to find and maintain it each mile. Take a moment to find good posture before every exercise, and every run, to optimize the way you move, and beat the clock.

Core stability has been beaten to death by the fitness world. Your core is not a singular part you'll find in Netter's anatomy textbook. And you don't (effectively) strengthen it just by doing crunches. Rather, it's a system of parts wired together to form a stable foundation so that the muscles that attach above and around it can actually do their work. Your joints feel position, your muscles create tension, and your neuromuscular system must be trained to coordinate movement in a running-specific manner.

This feedback loop doesn't exist solely in your abdominal wall, but in every place you move. In fact every joint has a core—a system of stabilizing muscles and mover muscles. And we'll ensure that you have a solid foundation at each joint before we get you moving.

Now that we have a plan to address the stiffness that pulls us into poor position, and have practiced finding and feeling your neutral spine, we need to teach the body how to integrate and stabilize the upper and lower body together. We want to make sure to train the ability to move the hips and shoulders without crumpling the can. Because running requires dynamic stability, not just static stability, there are no isometrics or planks in the precision movement workouts. We learn through movement, so let's get moving and learn to move better.

▷ WIRING POSTURE

FINGERTIP POSTURE DRILL

- Review the Posture Check (p. 210) to practice finding your neutral spine.

- Once you are in a neutral position, spread your fingers. Place your pinkies on the large bump in the front of your pelvis (your anterior superior iliac spine, or ASIS) and place your thumbs on any rib.

- Imagine your hands are vice grips locking your upper body position down over your pelvis and walk forward. Allow your thumbs and pinky fingers to cue your posture to remain stacked. Incorporate this drill throughout the day to build awareness, and even while running, using one hand to cue you into better alignment.

TIP

This may be the simplest cue to ensure your new core control transfers into your gait. The goal is to extend your hip behind you while keeping your torso stacked over your hips.

DON'T CRUSH YOUR CAN

When walking and running, many people extend the hip behind them, arch their back, and allow their ribs to flare upward.

REACH OUT

- Kneel and hold the handles of a suspension trainer, keeping your shoulders down and back. Lean forward into the rope.

- Reach your arms out overhead as far as you can without shrugging your shoulders. Keep your shoulder blades flat along your ribs.

- Hold your spine stable, and if you feel any increase in pelvic tilt or low back arch at all, adjust the setup: Place a foam roller under both shins (just below your knees), and keep your toes hovering off the floor. The slight instability in the foam roller will help you maintain your spine position as you reach outward.

- Do 3 sets of 10 reps.

TIP

To make this exercise easier, adjust the sling to be higher so that the angle of your body is less horizontal at full extension. To make it harder, lower the sling so that your body is more horizontal at full extension.

DONKEY TOES

- Begin on all fours with your thumbs pointing forward and your fingers pointing out to the sides. Come up onto your hands and toes, keeping your arms and thighs perpendicular to the ground (like a human coffee table).

- Maintaining a stable spine, lift one thigh toward the ceiling while keeping your knee bent to 90 degrees.

- Return to all fours and repeat with the opposite leg.

- Build to 2 minutes of alternating continuous movement.

TIP
If you need to build up gradually, start off with 4 sets of 30 seconds to learn proper movement.

BEAR WALK

- Once again, start on all fours, then come up on your hands and toes.

- Keep your back flat like a tabletop and walk forward with the opposite arm and leg (e.g., right hand goes with left foot).

- Take 30 steps forward and 30 steps backward.

The Secret of Counter-Rotation

While we run forward, running challenges us, and demands control in all three dimensions: front to back, side to side, and twisting. The concept of twisting force is not talked about much in the running world, but it is critically important. An ancient tribal toy, a pellet drum, illustrates why.

If you hold the drum and twist the handle equally in each direction, the beads at the end of the line on each side will swing, beating the drum on both sides in perfect synchronization. But if we bend the handle a bit then twist it, the beads hit out of sync. Instead of the fluid reciprocal energy exchange that we saw previously, there is now a block in the system. And everything wobbles.

This helps us understand the concept of the free moment. As you run forward, a line of twisting energy runs through your entire body. When your foot contacts the ground, this rotational energy is trying to twist your trunk, hip, and foot inward. Under ideal conditions, you show up with the skilled control to match this energy and steer your parts straight. It's Newton's third law, involving equal and opposite reactions. Yes, running requires twisting.

Counter-rotation allows the body to maintain a relatively smooth course as you run forward. But sometimes the pellet drum doesn't move smoothly. Maybe it's a result of your stiff foot, which won't adapt to the ground, or maybe you have poor coordination of your spinal rotation. Ultimately, a block in the body doesn't allow it to twist properly. And when we can't twist, we get kicked laterally, which causes the normal forces of 10–15 percent body weight to increase as much as 2–3 times the normal load. This instability makes running much harder than it should be, and it plays a big role in instability injuries throughout the body. It doesn't have to be this way.

Let's ensure that each joint has the necessary range of motion to twist and the stability to control it so you can run forward without getting kicked too far to either side. Specifically, we need to ensure that you can:

1. Twist the spine
2. Steer from the hip
3. Adapt the foot

▷ TWIST THE SPINE

Rotational control through the spine is a great way to sequence the core muscles. These muscles don't necessarily have to be strong, but they need to move us with intent: producing the right amount of control at the right time. When runners are told to rotate their spines, the overwhelming majority of them will move their spines into a side bend. If you haven't wired a pattern to be able to twist your spine on command, your body will never be able to find this rotation when running. The crunches and planks that runners are told to focus on don't help solve this problem. By targeting rotation you can ensure that your core is working in tandem with the rest of your body, not in isolation. And it creates a more stable spine, which is healthy for both your discs and joints, reducing the risk of injury.

FIGURE 6.1 You Twist When You Run
Counter-rotation helps to stabilize the body for more efficient running.

TWISTED WARRIOR

- From standing, drop into a high lunge. Position both hands on the floor inside your forward foot. Make sure the back leg is extended straight behind you.

- Raise your outside hand off the floor and twist your upper body, reaching your arm up toward the ceiling. Twist your trunk, not just your arms and head. Hold for a count of one.

- Untwist your body, and place your hand back on the floor. Repeat with the opposite arm.

- Twist 10 times in total (5 times on each side), then lunge on the other leg and repeat.

TIP

Imagine you have a camera on your chest, and the goal is to twist the camera all the way to the left and the right to take a picture of the people on either side of you. If you just force your arms into a twist, you won't get the photo.

MEDBALL TWIST

- Lie on your back with your knees bent at a 90-degree angle.

- Hold a medicine ball (5–15 lbs.) in both hands and keep your lower body relatively still as you rotate the ball, your torso, and head over to one side.

- Continue moving the ball from one side to the other, keeping your head relaxed on the floor through the movement, with both arms mostly straight.

- Do 40 reps to each side for a total of 80 reps.

BALL BRIDGE TWIST

- Lie on a Swiss ball so that your head and shoulders are resting on the ball, your knees are at a 90-degree angle, and your feet are shoulder-width apart on the floor. Keep your body—shoulders, hips, and knees—in bridge position.

- Raise your arms toward the ceiling and interlace your fingers.

- Roll your arms, torso, and head over to one side, then the other.

TIPS

Make sure your back stays quiet and that your glutes are working to keep your spine high.

If you feel any tension in your back, drop your hips slightly. Continue alternating from one side to the other for 2 minutes.

SWISS BALL TUCK TWIST

- Place your hands on the floor in push-up position (thumbs pointing forward and fingers out), and balance your shins on a Swiss ball.

- Tuck your legs under your body so that your hips lift up toward the ceiling. Holding this position, twist your torso to rotate the ball as far as you can go from left to right with a controlled movement.

- Do 3 sets of 30 seconds on, 30 seconds off.

TIP
Throughout the rotation, keep your hips and knees bent at 90 degrees as if you are sitting in a chair.

BUTT SCOOTS

■ Sit on the floor with your legs extended. Try to sit at a 90-degree angle so that your low back and pelvis are straight and not rounded.

■ Clasp your hands together and extend them in front of you, pushing your shoulders down and away from your ears.

■ Keep your upper body still, hike up one hip, and twist it forward so that your leg moves forward. Then hike and twist the opposite hip.

■ Do 3 sets of 10 times moving forward (5 scoots on each side), and then 10 times backward.

TIP

Imagine that you are trying to lengthen your legs by twisting from the hips, and taking steps with your sit bones instead of your feet.

SUPER SWISS SIDE PLANK

- Lie on your side and hold a Swiss ball between your feet.

- Prop yourself up on your elbow and draw your shoulder blade back and down along your ribcage for support.

- Raise your hips so that your upper body is parallel to the floor, then lower to start position.

- Do 25 reps on each side.

TIP

The challenge here is to keep the pulsing movement in a lateral plane, without twisting down to the floor.

THREAD THE NEEDLE PLANK

- Anchor a TheraBand to a point that is a few inches to a foot from the floor. Get into a plank position with your arms extended and the band perpendicular to your body. Your feet should be slightly wider than shoulder-width.

- Support your upper body with the arm closest to the band's attachment point, and reach your opposite hand under your chest to grab the band.

- Now untwist your spine into a plank position, tucking the shoulder blade back along your ribs, and extend the arm holding the band to the side until it is straight and parallel to the floor.

- Return the band to its attachment point and repeat.

- Do 20 reps on each side.

TIP

The majority of the twist should occur in the upper body while the lower body remains still.

LONG ARM BAND SQUAT

- Attach a Powerband to a point that is between chest and waist height and stand perpendicular to the band. Position yourself far enough from the attachment point to create tension in the band.

- Set your feet just wider than hip width, hold the band in both hands, and extend your shoulders out in front. The tension on the band should twist your body inward.

- Counter this by twisting back against the band enough to hold your upper and lower body square as you squat up and down.

- Do 20 reps on each side

TIPS

If your knees are moving too far forward or your back is rounding, place a chair behind you and squat down until you touch it.

Step closer to the attachment point to ease the load and farther away to increase the load.

HANG SPINE TWIST

- Hang from a pull-up bar with your arms relaxed. Bend your hips and knees up as if you are sitting in a chair.

- Try to keep your belly button still and do a side bend, reaching your right hip toward your right shoulder, then your left hip up to your left shoulder. Keep the sway of your body to a minimum.

- Do 25 reps on each side for a total of 50 reps.

▷ STEER FROM THE HIP

Sure, muscles in the hips drive the body forward, but they also play a huge role in injury prevention as they steer the path of the leg. This rotation doesn't just influence the hip; it helps control the position of the knee and foot as well. Some people say the gluteus maximus is the best orthotic money can buy.

GLUTE RAINBOW

- Start on all fours, with your thumbs pointing forward and your fingers pointing to the sides. Imagine there is a plumb bob hanging from your chest—keep it still as you start the movement.

- Lift one leg behind you so that your thigh is horizontally aligned with your torso and your knee is bent at 90 degrees with the sole of your foot pointing to the ceiling.

- Keeping your thigh at the exact same height and your pelvis level, twist your hip out so that you make a rainbow and the inside of the foot points inward.

- Keep your spine stable and twist the leg back outward to complete one rep.

- Do 10 reps on each side.

TIP

Don't let your low back arch or shift. The only joint moving is the hip.

BANDED HIP TWIST

- Anchor a TheraBand at waist height, stand square to the band, and pull the band around your pelvis so that it sits just below your waist.

- Put your hands on your hips, holding the band in place with some tension on it.

- Stand on the leg where the band ends (if the band wraps around from the right, stand on your left leg) and rotate your pelvis in and out while keeping your hips level.

- Do 40 reps on each side.

TIP

Step closer to the attachment to ease the load and farther away to increase the load.

STANDING HIP CIRCLES

- Place your hands on your hips and lift one knee so that your thigh is parallel to the floor and your knee is bent at 90 degrees in front of you.

- Move your leg out to the side.

- While keeping your knee at the same height, twist your foot behind you while keeping the pelvis level.

TIP

Pay attention to the position of your hands on your hips to keep your back still.

- Push your leg straight back so the sole of your foot points behind you.

- Bring your hip back into center, and then back to the floor. This is one rep. Each part of the movement should be specific and deliberate.

- Do 5 reps on each side, alternating left and right.

The band loops around the backside of your hip, to be anchored with the hand on the same side as your stance leg.

BANDED TIPPY BIRD

- Building rotational control in a hinge position is critical as the muscles in the hip change their leverage as compared to holding a vertical torso.

- You can stand on flat ground, but standing on a MOBO will train you to build distinct control through both the foot and hips. Fins go in the OUTER slots 3+4.

- Loop a resistance band under your RIGHT foot, drop into a hinge, and then pull it TIGHT as you wrap it around the outside of your opposite hip. Anchor the band on the same side as your stance leg. Use your free hand for balance support.

- Let the tension in the band twist your pelvis inward and then twist your pelvis as high as you can outward. Aim for full motion in your hips.

- Do 25 reps on each side.

- Building rotational control in a hinge position, where your hip muscles need to change their leverage, will result in strength and stability to benefit you when you are vertical.

TIP
Start with a light band and focus on using all the internal and external range of motion you have in your hips. As you build full control, load this movement with a heavier resistance band.

ROTISSERIE CHICKEN

- Lie on your back and place one leg in the suspension trainer, with the strap just below your knee. Extend your free leg next to the sling leg. Lift your hips into a bridge and extend your arms above your chest, palms together.

- On the sling side, keep your kneecap pointed up to the ceiling and rotate your pelvis away on an imaginary axis, as if you were on a BBQ spit.

- Rotate back inward past the start position. The hips should twist fully inward and fully outward each rep—your back stays quiet and your hands remain extended above you.

- Do 2 sets of 8 reps on each side.

TIPS

Pay attention to whether you are twisting equally to the right and left sides.

If you feel any tightness in your low back, drop your chest slightly until it dissipates.

▷ ADAPT THE FOOT

Your foot is not a brick. It's a leaf spring with the ability to twist and adapt to the ground to keep you stable. For this to happen, it is critical that your forefoot and rearfoot have good mobility and that motion between your forefoot and rearfoot is specifically controlled by the muscles inside the foot. So let's get to it. The first thing you must do is screw the big toe to the ground without cheating motion through your rearfoot.

Pronation and Supination

It's time to bust the single-biggest myth to dominate running vocabulary in recent decades. I'm here to tell you once and for all that you don't *overpronate* or *oversupinate*.

You have body parts that move. Your spine flexes back and forth. Your hips twist, moving in and out and front to back. Your knees move back and forth and your ankle pushes you forward. *And your foot moves too...in pronation and supination.*

These are neutral terms. People don't get intimidated by words like "bend," "flex," or "twist"—so why do we get wound up about pronating and supinating?

I think it's mostly a misunderstanding. We tend to think in global terms—we move forward, turn, and cut sideways. Those are clear directions that we can wrap our heads around, and most body parts follow such a path. But feet are different because they have lots of bones, 26 to be exact. And the main axis in which they adapt to the ground isn't oriented straight ahead, but rather in a diagonal about 45 degrees out to the side and about 15 degrees up off the floor. Since the axis of the joint is shifted quite a bit off of a straight, planar motion, feet don't move in one absolute plane of motion, but through all three planes at once. And this movement is called pronation and supination. These words simply describe the motion; they aren't negative or critical in any way.

Let's look beyond running. Rock climbers adapt their hands to the surface of the rock in various ways to establish a firm contact point. We don't call this "overgripping." Likewise, when walking, running, cutting, and jumping you don't "overpronate" as your foot adapts to the ground—*you move your foot enough to get a solid foundation.*

I've been at this for 20 years. There were many research studies that came before me. *There isn't solid research establishing a powerful connection between the amount of foot motion (pronation/supination) and injury or performance.* Period.

But if you are a rock climber and you can't produce enough force to hold onto the rock, you will go tumbling down. You failed to control your connection point, and that's clearly a bad thing. Likewise, If you are walking, running, cutting, and jumping on your feet and you can't control how quickly and forcefully you pronate and supinate in your feet, that can lead to tissue overload, which is bad as well. Research does support findings that the rate of pronation and supination in your feet, and how this influences body parts up the chain, does matter.

So let's stop stressing about foot motion and these terms. The amount of pronation in your foot is fine. It's how well you control it that's key. You need to control the motion in your knee just like you need to control the motion in your feet. Let's ensure that we build solid skill for better foot control. Train your feet to improve run speed and jumping ability, and reduce injury risk all the way up the chain.

Foot Mobility Test

- Stand on one foot and close your eyes. What happens? Where does your balance shift? While it's normal to wobble a little, your weight should be evenly balanced across the ball of your foot from the inside to the outside.

- Now stand on the opposite foot. Your feet may move quite differently, so don't be alarmed if your balance strategy is different from one side to the other.

If you notice a tendency to drift laterally to the outside of your foot		You likely have a soft tissue forefoot varus. This is caused by a tight lateral band in the plantar fascia that tries to pull your big toe up off the floor. If so, the forefoot varus mobility exercise that follows will release it to improve the contact your big toe makes with the floor.
If you noted even pressure across the foot while standing		There is no need to perform this mobility correction.
If you were exceptionally wobbly		We'll tackle that problem by improving your foot coordination with the toe yoga and our single-leg exercises later in the chapter.

Step 1: Get your big toe down to the ground

FOREFOOT VARUS MOBILITY

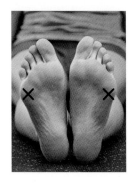

- Stand with a lacrosse ball under your fourth and fifth metatarsals (just behind the ball of the foot) with your heel in contact with the floor. Turn both feet into a slight pigeon toe position, and softly bend your knees.

- Put your hands on your hips and rotate your pelvis and trunk right and left for about 90 seconds. The ball should not move at all under your foot; instead focus on twisting your body above the ball.

If you drifted laterally in the foot mobility test, this area of the foot will feel quite sore during the forefoot varus mobility exercise. It's okay to push through the soreness, but try to allow the foot to relax. When you take your foot off the ball and stand on one leg, you should notice a considerable difference. The foot should feel flatter from outside to inside, and it should be easier to use your big toe for control. After 2 or 3 weeks of doing this exercise, the plantar fascia should unwind, giving you a flatter foot position and less discomfort. Once you feel the change you don't need to continue doing the correction. Just stand on one foot to do a simple self-check prior to a run or a Running Rewired workout. If your foot feels flat from inside to outside, proceed. But if you feel shifted to the outside, do the corrective exercise first.

Step 2: Control your big toe independently of your other toes

Once your big toe is on the ground, it's time to improve the coordination of the muscles that stabilize the twist between the forefoot and rearfoot. The main reasons that runners move excessively inside their feet has nothing to do with foot type (high arch versus low arch), and everything to do with how you control your foot type. Normally, the big toe provides about 85 percent of the stability in your foot. If you can't master the coordination of the big toe, it's a forefoot problem. And when you've got a forefoot problem, the arch and rearfoot are unsupported and collapse down. This problem is typically the cause of symptoms in Achilles, plantar fascia, metatarsals, shins, and almost any other foot and lower leg pain. Targeting the forefoot is the solution to keep the foot and lower leg aligned during running.

Foot Control Test

- Stand on both feet, but focus on only one foot at a time. Raise your big toe while leaving the four little toes flat on the ground, then drive your big toe straight down (without curling it) and elevate the other toes.

- As you push your big toe down the arch of your foot will rise up slightly. Make sure you can drive the big toe down without collapsing the position of your arch and ankle to cheat the movement.

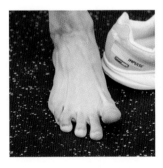 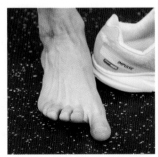 

If you can't perform this test correctly, practice this movement, which I call Toe Yoga, as a corrective exercise.

If you found that you collapsed your arch to get your big toe down	Place the heel of your shoe perpendicular to the inside of your ankle to provide a visual to ensure you learn to move the big toe without cheating your foot and ankle position. Practice this movement until you learn the pattern.
If you have trouble raising your big toe	We need to clean up your control. Position a ruler under your big toe so that the end of the ruler is beneath the ball of your foot. Raise the end of the ruler so that it lifts your toe upward. Hold the free end of the ruler so it provides a little resistance, and push your toe straight down, isolating the muscles around the big toe. Imagine you are pushing the toe and ruler through the floor. If you see the joint inside the big toe bending, you are cheating the movement with a muscle in your shin. Deliberate practice will create specific control of the big toe for improved balance and foot control.

This movement builds a tripod for better foot control. It's worth talking about triangles for a moment. A lot of people talk about the tripod of the foot as being from the heel to each side of the ball of the foot. But your foot is never static on the ground when running, and that analogy doesn't match the demands of running. A research study I personally led showed that the foot is most loaded AFTER the heel comes off the ground. You've likely heard the riddle: "What puts more force down to the ground per square area: an elephant or a woman wearing high heels?" Sure the elephant is heavy, but the enormous weight is dissipated through the enormous foot. Conversely, the small pinpoint tip of the high heel puts a lot of weight of the much lighter woman in one small location. When running, only the tripod of the forefoot—the inner and outer ball of the foot, and the end of your big toe—is in contact to actively control and stabilize the twisting load within your foot. We need to train you to control the line of force transfer within your foot and train feet to move. When you notice instability on one leg, it's common to focus on the wobble, which leads to frustration and more instability. Instead, focus on the solution. Building this tripod will build a better foundation for all of the single-leg exercises in this program and for your run.

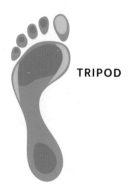

TRIPOD

Step 3: Screw your foot down while screwing your hip out

Many runners have been told to use their big toe, and so they collapse their foot inward, which in turn collapses their knee and hip. Other runners have been told to fire their glutes, which often leads them to roll the foot up and out, losing foot contact in the process. Both situations are problematic. Our goal is to ground the big toe to support the foot while simultaneously engaging the external rotators in the hips.

FOAM ROLLER DRILL

- Stand with a foam roller between your shins. Squeeze it tightly so that your big toes are grounded and active as they press down through the floor.

- Now place your hands on your glutes and squeeze them tight. Feel them engage as you screw the hips out and then back in while you keep the toe grounded and maintain inward pressure on the roller.

- Practice this motion for about 1–2 minutes or until you can move smoothly.

TIP

This might feel odd, but this twisting builds the link between your foot and hips to steer your legs straight for healthy alignment while running. Once this skill becomes easy, you can translate it into more complex exercises.

TIPPY TWIST

- Place your hands on your hips and balance on one leg, focusing on a strong tripod through the forefoot.

- Maintain a neutral spine and keep your hips level as you bend forward, extending the nonsupporting leg behind you.

- Twist your hips in toward the floor, then out and up toward the ceiling. Keep your weight balanced across the middle of your foot as you pivot from the hip.

- Return to level hips and the pelvis forward to come back up to starting position. That's one full rep.

- Perform 2 sets of 10 reps on each foot.

TIPS

If you wobble in your foot, focus on grounding the big toe to solidify the inside of the tripod.

You learn balance through successful movement. It's better to twist the hip through a smaller range with good control than to try to twist too far and fall each time.

To regress this exercise, place one hand on a chair or wall to help improve your movement quality.

If you master this movement, progress it by standing on a MOBO with fins in the even slots.

The exercises in this chapter are focused on precision movement. Rotational control is probably not something you have on your radar, but it's a key strategy to improving your running. These movements help to wire intramuscular control in your spine, hips, and feet to improve intermuscular control through the entire body. It epitomizes the age-old saying that the whole is greater than the sum of its parts. Deliberate practice will build the skill you need to move safely, so take your time with these exercises, move with purpose, and build a solid foundation to combat the rotational demands of running.

MOBO: A Tool for Success

Over my career, I noticed a huge black hole in how runners train. We train the core, hips, and knees though the full range of motion required for running, but we don't go below the sockline. Why not train the feet? Embarrassingly, the gold standard for foot and ankle care has been moving your foot back and forth with a band. In no way do these movements train your foot for the demands of running. Maybe you saw a PT who is a "running specialist," and they had you doing towel curls or marble pick-ups. These exercises have two significant flaws. First, they train the muscles in the shin, not the foot. Second, they train you to raise the ball of your foot off the ground each and every rep as your toes curl. This motion is not part of your walking and running gait. We need to stop reinforcing nonfunctional movement skill.

Eventually I developed my own set of foot-specific exercises that worked quite well, but the movement was nuanced, and people would come back doing the exercise incorrectly. I wanted runners to have a tool to feel and figure out proper foot control. It was a long process of prototypes and testing that ultimately led to a new tool for runners. The MOBO (mobility board) was designed around the way your body moves naturally, with the goal of solving three key problems.

1. To train the feet for the motion required in running. You run forward, but the axis of motion in which feet adapt to the ground is not straight, but at a diagonal. The adjustable fins on MOBO allow you to build control through the normal motions of pronation and supination, and they can be moved to target different movement strategies and tissue loading.

2. To drive the big toe down with force and control. When runners drive their big toe down for support they typically end up curling their toes and gripping, which never happens in walking, running, and jumping. The board has a cutout for the little toes that prevents curling and gripping, and further cues you to engage the muscles in the big toe and arch to control the movement of the board.

3. To integrate the movement of the foot and body. You are a person, not just a foot. MOBO loads your foot in a weight-bearing position that teaches you how to sync your foot with your entire body for running.

Fin Location	Target
Even Slots	Arch to support your feet
Odd Slots	Outer shin to anchor your big toe down
Forward Slots	Calf to increase achilles tendon strength
Outer Slots	Arch to stabilize the foot and fix ankle sprains
Backward Slots	Foot as you load the knee in squats

FOOT ROCKS

▪ Place the board right side up, insert the fins from the bottom into the even slots, and step on the board. (To do this exercise you will train with both the even and odd fin positions on each foot.)

▪ While standing with your ribs stacked over your hips, drive the toe side of the board down to the ground, then the heel side. This is one rep. Repeat this for 20 reps total.

▪ Remove the fins and insert them into the odd slots from the bottom with the right side still face-up. Do 20 reps to finish working the right leg.

▪ Now flip the board over so that the left side is up and repeat this entire sequence with your left foot. Do 20 reps with fins in the even slots and 20 reps in the odd slots.

TIPS

To control rocking visualize eggshells below both sides of the board and move in a way that would tap–not smash them.

If this exercise is too challenging, place one hand on a wall or chair to get stability in your trunk and improve the control in your foot.

Note: This exercise (and the banded version that follows) improves stability in the foot and ankle. The #6 precision workout includes both variations in a single session. To do these on your own to build strength, alternate between exercises with each session.

BANDED FOOT ROCKS

- Banded foot rocks load the motion occurring in your feet. The only difference from the Foot Rock exercise is that the resistance band is looped through the slot in the board. So if the fins are in the even slots, the band is looped through the #1 slot.

- Step onto the MOBO with the right side up and fins in the even slots. Loop the band through the #1 slot and hold it in your left hand.

- Drive the board down so that the front edge taps the ground and then tap the back of the board in a controlled forward-and-back movement. This is one rep. Do 20 reps on your right leg.

- Keep the right side of the board face-up and place the fins into the odd slots, looping the band through the #4 slot. Do 20 more reps to finish training your right leg.

- Now flip the board over to repeat the same sequence on your left leg.

TIP

As you load the motion in your feet, ensure you keep your trunk quiet as you rock the board back and forth.

FOOT BAND TWIST

- To work the right foot, place the fins in the even slots and put the MOBO on the floor right side up. Position the board to be right of the band attachment (i.e., the band will be coming from the left).

- Place your right foot on the board with your big toe on the board and the others hovering inside the toe box. Your left knee will be bent with your foot in the air.

- Grab the exercise band in both hands and press it out in front of you with your arms extended straight.

- Press your big toe down to keep the MOBO totally still and level as you twist toward and away from the band attachment point. Keep your motion minimal, moving your entire upper body so as not to exceed shoulder-width to the right and left. Do 30 reps.

- Now switch to work the opposite foot. Position the left side of the board face up, and place the fins in the even slots. The band will be anchored to your right. Do 30 additional reps.

TIPS

As you twist, imagine a skewer running through your spine, but don't lean sideways. This movement builds up muscles in your arch and trains rotational control in your feet.

If it seems too difficult, wrap the band around the end of a broom or ski pole, and hold all of it in your hands. This provides a pivot point to build rotational control with added stability.

EVERTED PASS BACK

- Place the MOBO right side up with fins in the outside slots (3, 4). The board will not rock—it will remain stationary. As you step onto the board, you'll notice that the outer part of your foot is high and the inner part of your foot is low.

- Hold a kettlebell and pass it back and forth between your hands for 2 minutes.

- This continual motion helps to break the habit of shifting your weight outward as you focus on keeping weight on the inside of your foot to push your arch up.

- Now flip the board over and perform the same movement up for 2 minutes on your left leg.

TIPS

This exercise anchors the inside of your foot to kick your arch into the game. It's also very helpful if you tend to roll your ankles a lot.

Take breaks as needed to maintain quality movement.

STAR SQUAT

- Position the MOBO right side up, with fins in the even slots. Step into a loop of a resistance band.

- Place your right foot on the board and your hands on your hips to cue level hips throughout the squats, which are only quarter squats—no need to go deep with these.

- Perform a mini squat, extending your left leg forward to just above the ground, and come back up. Do a mini squat, extending your left leg laterally, and come back up. Do a final mini squat, extending the leg behind you. These three movements are counted as one rep. Do a total of 5 reps (which is 15 mini squats per set).

- Do 2 sets of 5 reps on each leg, taking a break between each set.

TIP

While squatting up and down, it's important that your feet and hips steer the leg straight.

The exercises in this chapter are focused on precision movement. Rotational control is probably not something you have on your radar, but it's a key strategy to improving your running. These movements help to wire intramuscular control in your spine, hips, and feet to improve intermuscular control through the entire body. It epitomizes the age-old saying that the whole is greater than the sum of its parts. Deliberate practice will build the skill you need to move safely, so take your time with these exercises, move with purpose, and build a solid foundation to combat the rotational demands of running.

Push for Better Propulsion

When you run, about half the effort for propulsion comes from elasticity stored in your tendons, and half comes from muscle. But to use that elasticity and muscle force wisely, you need to harness the power of triple extension—driving simultaneously from the hip, knee, and ankle. We need to build this pattern reflexively for it to transfer into your running form.

The skill of triple extension is often thwarted by our lifestyle. We spend so much time with our legs in front of us: sitting, driving, cycling, squatting, etc. This means runners have no trouble swinging their leg out in front of their body. Conversely, very few things we do require us to drive our leg behind our body. Simply running more will not develop this skill—it takes practice. Running requires you to swing your leg behind you. And not just passively, but powerfully.

FIGURE 7.1 Triple Extension Pushes You Forward
Triple extension is simultaneously driving the leg behind the body from the hip, knee, and ankle.

A lack of triple extension shifts your stride. In Chapter 4, we established that every runner contacts slightly ahead of their body when running at a steady speed. Doing so allows you to "load the spring," much like pulling back on a sling shot before you fire the rock. The length of your stride should equate to equal time storing energy with your leg in front of you, and equal time releasing it behind you. However, a lack of leg drive forces most runners to make contact too far out in front their body, throwing off this balance. Sure, you are still able to run, but the metabolic cost is higher, and the load distributed at each joint becomes problematic. Instead of your muscles working together from the midstance to push-off phases of your gait, a different pattern emerges.

Runners who fail to execute triple extension exhibit excessive vertical motion, increased knee bend in the stance phase, a failure to drive their hip into extension, a flexed knee at push-off, and excessive loading in their calf complex. Ultimately, this pattern swaps horizontal displacement (which creates propulsion) in exchange for vertical displacement (which amounts to wasted energy). It's no surprise the runner will fatigue more quickly.

Overstriding Overloads the Body

Overstriding shifts the entire dynamic of your run. It doesn't just affect the total load on your body—it also affects how the work of running is distributed to each of your joints. Contacting too far in front of your body creates tissue overload and compromises economy too.

First things first: Overstriding can wreck your knees. Nearly every study on running injuries ranks patella-femoral pain in the top three injuries ailing runners. Your patella, or kneecap, basically functions as a pulley for your quad. When you overstride, the torque or mechanical load on the knee is greater. This creates more shear across the surface of the patella, which is detrimental to the long-term health of the cartilage underneath it.

Overstriding can also lead to increased mechanical demand in the foot and ankle. When you land too far ahead of center, your foot and ankle demand more control as they adapt to the ground. If you can decrease your overstride, you can decrease the tissue strain in the lower leg and foot. As an example, you must lower the foot down to the ground, which works muscles in the front of the shin and inside of the shin and foot to allow the foot to adapt under control. Overstriding places more stress and strain on the muscles, bones, and tendons in this region.

Third, there are some performance implications in terms of elasticity and muscle work. As a rule of thumb, whenever we can delegate the work required in a task between more muscles, we are on a path to improving efficiency. When runners overstride, more work is directed toward the quads, which are home to a greater percentage of fast-twitch fibers. So for a given running pace, your quads will be working closer to peak capacity and enter into a fatigued, or an acidic, state sooner. When muscle gets too acidic, the pH level drops and the muscle can't contract and relax as well, so you end up hitting the wall. Since the glute has more slow-twitch fibers, it produces smaller amounts of acidic waste products and can last longer before building up a lot of waste. This means you can drill the pace a bit harder and longer without falling apart.

The lab data I've collected over a decade reveals why the vast majority of runners don't know how to fully use the muscles in their backside. It would be much easier if muscle control was balanced around the body, but the reality is most people are out of balance, a problem that is not exclusive to running. Dr. Vladimir Janda, a pioneer in muscular therapy, coined the term "lower crossed syndrome" to describe the imbalance that occurs when the hip flexors, quads, and low back muscles are tight and overused, and the deep core and glute max are asleep at the wheel.

A lot of running gurus and social media trolls claim that this imbalance is simple to fix: you just have to increase your cadence. Yes, increasing your cadence can help reduce loads at the knee, ankle, and foot. So can trying to contact a little bit closer to your body. But over the years the narrow focus on a shorter stride or faster turnover results in a lot of runners who are just taking a bunch of short-to-tiny steps, which is not the most efficient way to run.

Their overstride was a result of their muscle memory and body control. Thus, to change the stride, we need to change the dynamic. If you

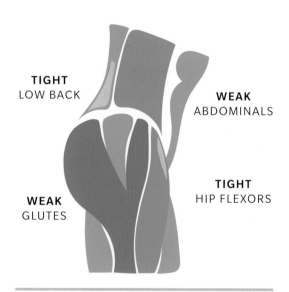

FIGURE 7.2 Lower Crossed Syndrome
Most people are movement-dominant with the low back, quads, and hip flexors. We need to maximize the recruitment of the opposite diagonal to tap into the core and glute max.

really want to create the type of changes that will keep your form in check whether you are fresh or fatigued, changing your muscle dominance is the best way to reduce stress per stride and optimize your energy cost of running. We are going to switch our focus from big picture to a joint-by-joint approach. Here's what your lower-body joints need to bring to the table to optimize your triple extension.

JOINT-BY-JOINT FUNCTION

The hips

There's a lot of variability in people, and variability in running form. But as a physio who has spent thousands of hours in a biomechanics lab, I frequently joke about "things people should be able to do." As a runner, you should be able to move, stabilize, and load your hips without compromising your spine position. To build a solid hip drive, you need adequate mobility to get your hip behind your body, muscle control to guide your leg straight, and the ability to properly drive your hips behind you.

HIP MOBILITY: Remember the best way to inhibit the muscles around your hips is to screw up your posture. And then there's the issue of tight hips. If those muscles are tight, your hip won't have full extension to both sides of your pelvis. This imbalance isn't a running problem; it's a body problem. If this body problem isn't corrected, you'll never be able to correct your stride. About 80 percent of runners have hip mobility restrictions that compound their posture and their stride. Use the hip mobility test in Chapter 5 to see if you need to improve your hip flexor length, and if so, take action. Should you pass the test, the Twisted Warrior exercise in Chapter 6 is a great pre-run move to keep those hips moving at your peak pre-run.

HIP DRIVE AND STEERING: Your glute max has three primary functions, all of which benefit your running. First and foremost, the glute max is an incredibly powerful, fatigue-resistant, extensor of the hip joint. Extensors are the muscles that drive your hip from the front side to the backside of your body. As we run forward, these extensors generate the push to drive us past our foot plant on the ground. The muscles on the backside of the body move us in ways that the muscles on the front side can't replicate. The glutes don't act alone to move the hip—the hamstrings help out as well. But while the glutes and hamstrings both move the hip, the glute's architecture allows it to provide two critical elements of stability that the hamstrings can't match.

Your glute max is also your primary hip external rotator. People often show me photos of themselves running with their knees crashing in, a problem that they attribute to a weak glute medius. In theory, the glute medius muscle pulls laterally on the outside of the hip to keep the knee from collapsing inward. However, this is an oversimplification that can lead you to waste time targeting a smaller, less powerful muscle.

A recent study set out to look at the role of the glute medius and measure the path of the knee in walking and running. The researchers anesthetized the nerve that tells the glute medius to fire. This shut it off completely. Then they asked people to walk and run, expecting to see massive knee collapse to the inside—but that didn't happen. That's because muscles don't work in isolation. We move as a system. That two-dimensional knee collapse that you see in photos isn't really a two-dimensional collapse.

In my lab, I measure both the motion of the frontal plane (in-to-out motion) and rotational plane (twist) of the hip. When a runner's knees dive in, I don't see significantly different frontal plane numbers, but there are significant differences in the rotational plane. Thus, that 2D frontal plane problem is really more of a 3D rotational problem. Better rotational control from the glute max will keep your leg from twisting inward and keep it tracking correctly. Most importantly, your nervous system can only generate maximum force when it feels stable. If you can get the stabilizing muscles around your hips to show up to steer the leg straight, your propulsion will be at full throttle.

Finally, your glute max also plays a huge role in postural control. In Chapter 5 we used a can metaphor to understand how posture problems happen. The glute max is anchored to the bottom of this can and attaches below the hip. If it's firing correctly, it will keep the can upright by pulling it straight. If the glute max is shut off, the entire can will pitch forward. And as soon as the can starts tipping forward, everything falls apart. The exaggerated forward lean forces you into a huge overstride, which makes for very high loading rates, putting the body under more stress with every step. Don't assume that this is a problem only for overweight or oversized runners to worry about. The highest loading rate I've measured in my lab didn't involve a 280-pound Clydesdale athlete, but a 12-year-old girl who weighed 88 pounds. Each step was almost shaking the room. Her torso was pitched so far forward that her feet were forced to land really far in front of her body, delivering a huge amount of stress with every impact. We got her using her hips properly, and within two weeks she dropped her loading rate by 70 percent, back into normal territory and her pain disappeared. This stuff matters.

better booty = better posture

We need to break this lower-cross syndrome pattern and wire you to control a new pattern. You need a solid core to help your glute max work, yet you can see how a glute deficiency affects your posture and your core. It's a classic catch-22. This is why we don't train muscles to achieve this skill; we train movements. And you need to own this movement. You need to feel how much you can move your hips without your posture falling apart. And how does the position of your back influence the muscle demand of your hips? In terms of building this muscle memory, we'll use some intramuscular cues to help you find these muscles, but the critical step is to integrate these cues with intermuscular coordination. It's not isolation, but rather

GLUTE ON   **GLUTE INHIBITED**

FIGURE 7.3 Hip Drive and Posture
One major role of the glute max is to control postural orientation. If the glute is inhibited, it can't generate enough force to keep you upright. The torso tips forward, which leads to overstriding.

systemic coordination that produces long-term gains. Here's your new mantra: "Drive from the hips, keep the spine stable." Repeat this as you do all the exercises in this chapter . . . and think about it while running!

Finally, we know that flexibility does not equal mobility. Remember, flexibility is passive. Mobility is active. Just because you stretched your hip flexors doesn't mean that you've magically flipped the glute switch to "on" and changed your gait so you can start driving with your hips. The quad-dominant movement pattern most of us bring to running is strong, and Plan B has been reinforced by years of running. To regain Plan A, I'll teach you to stabilize into this new range. Once you figure out how to tap into your backside muscles, you'll stride less out front, and more out the back. This means you'll do less pulling yourself along, and more pushing yourself along.

The knees

Your knees primarily flex and extend front to back, and their primary job is to dampen the braking and vertical loads. During the flight phase, your body is a projectile soaring through the air. When your foot lands in front of your body each stride, the knee complex works hard to "smooth" this landing. It also helps drive vertical force down to the ground, which we'll learn more about in Chapter 10.

The quads and hamstrings are big muscles capable of producing a huge amount of force. No matter your form, these muscles need to show up ready to work. But muscles don't act alone, and we certainly don't want the quads

alone to carry the torch when running. We need to integrate your knees with your hip and ankle drive to ensure you get a solid push with every stride, one that holds up under fatigue.

The big muscles around the knee are anatomically set up to work, but since they are stuck between the hips and feet, they can be susceptible to middle-child syndrome. Their function is impacted by how effectively the muscles above and below are able to steer the leg straight. Yet again, stability impacts elasticity, and the performance of the knee can never be looked at as an isolated joint.

The feet

What happens below the knee is key. Remember that running is all about maximizing elasticity, and the achilles tendon is the biggest rubber band in your arsenal. The definition of "work" is applying force through a distance (W=F x D). As the achilles is a long, thick, and robust tendon it is able to store and release a lot of energy and thus it actually accounts for about half of the work required for propulsion every stride. There are two things you can do to optimize the elasticity in your achilles:

1. **Develop strong calf muscles:** If you hold a rubber band loose and limp, it can't store and release energy. When you pull it taut and hold the ends stable, you load and release the rubber band. The achilles tendon sits between your calf muscles and your heel bone. The calf muscle complex and achilles tendon experience loads of 5–7 times your body weight with every stride.

The calf muscles must be incredibly strong to keep the achilles tendon taut through the stance phase.

2. **Work on solid foot stability:** On the other side, the tendon inserts into your heel bone. Your heel bone is a pretty solid and robust structure, but the position of you heel bone is dependent on the 26 bones that make up your foot. Research has shown that poor control of the muscles in your arch can allow the position of your foot to twist excessively during the push-off phase, and thus compromise elasticity of that tendon. Further, fatigue in the calf muscles can compromise the elasticity in your tendon, and lead to overloading the muscles in your feet. Your foot's job is to steer the foot straight to keep the tendon at its right length. And the rotational control in the hips have a huge effect on the control of your feet as well. But don't stress about the details—this plan is comprehensive to ensure we cover all the bases. In Chapter 6 we focused on building better rotational control in your foot for a stable foundation. In Chapter 9 we'll highlight how to target a strong tendon, and the performance lifts and loaded carries will demand that your calf and achilles are primed for propulsion.

In summary, triple extension describes an integrated movement involving the 1) hips, 2) knees, and 3) ankles to create propulsion in running. We have looked at the function of each of these joints individually, but they need to be trained to fire together to maximize stability and elasticity for propulsion. The majority of exercises in this chapter target hip steering and hip drive to improve the function of your core, hips, knees, and, yes, even your feet.

You're Smarter Than That

"Your glutes aren't firing" is one of the most commonly used phrases by physicians, physios, and coaches these days. Let's not get lost in the semantics: This is not a hardware problem. The nerve that tells the glutes to fire is still plugged into your nervous system. And under voluntary command, you can get your butt muscles to kick on just fine.

However, remember optimal skill or strategy in your running form means that you reflexively fire your hip muscles in the right amount and at the right time to achieve triple extension. So in reality, what these experts are describing is that you aren't syncing your hip muscle activation with your central pattern generators in the correct way.

The Running Rewired plan aims to train proper muscle recruitment, and then integrate it into your running form.

▷ DRIVE FROM THE HIPS

PIGEON HIP EXTENSION

- Get into a pigeon position. Rest the knee of the leg extended behind you on the floor.

- Bring the forward leg horizontally below your torso and rest your lower leg on the floor. Use it to ensure you aren't cheating with your back—it is not necessary to drop low, even if you are quite flexible.

- Without moving your pelvis, tighten the glutes and raise your back knee off the floor and move your body into extension at the hip. Keep your back foot on the floor. Maintain tightness in the glute as you lower the knee back down to the floor.

- Do 40 reps on each side.

TIP

It's easy to contract a muscle and shorten it (to get your knee off the floor), but harder to lengthen it under contraction (lowering the knee down). Keep your glutes active during the entire movement.

FROG BRIDGE

- Lie on your back with your legs bent at roughly 90 degrees and the soles of your feet together, knees open. Clasp your hands together and extend your arms toward the ceiling.

- Press your hips up as high as possible without arching your back to engage the glute max.

- Do 50 reps.

CHAIR OF DEATH SQUAT

- Using your hands, hold a dowel vertically along your head, mid back, and tailbone. (The dowel ensures you keep a neutral spine and hinge from the hips, not the back.) Stand with your feet about 2 inches from the base of a box or chair.

- Keep the dowel in place and squat, making sure not to pull your body away from the critical points of contact.

- Perform 20 reps.

TIP

The box or chair will prevent your knees from moving too far forward and train you to move your hips backward, which cues the glutes and keeps the quads in check for a proper hip hinge.

FOCUS ON FORM

For those of you who are new to strength training, this is a critical exercise to develop the correct skill of squatting. Try to do a set of 15 reps before you do the performance workouts to ensure you build muscle memory, moving safely and getting the most from your training.

Kneecap Release

A lot of runners develop pain around the kneecap that is due to the connective tissue (the IT band, the quad tendon, and the retinaculum that binds your knee together) stiffening up and pulling the kneecap up too high. Instead of rolling and gliding in its groove, the kneecap pivots within the joint, which can lead to excessive wear and tear. Use this corrective exercise to improve mobility of the tissue above the kneecap so it can drop down and track as it should. Cut off the valve stem of an old mountain bike tube to make one long tube.

- Bend your knee at a 10-degree angle and place one end of the tube just above your knee.

- Wrap the tube around your thigh tightly, slowly working your way up the lower half of your thigh. Tuck the end of the tube into the wrapped section to secure it.

- Do 20 squats to full depth, making sure to fully straighten the knee at the top.

Unwrap your knee and do a test squat to see how you feel. If it helps, do this corrective exercise before your runs for a few weeks to unload the kneecap.

SINGLE-LEG DEADLIFT WITH DOWEL

- Stand on one leg, holding a dowel vertically along your back.

- Bend forward, making sure that you hold the dowel firmly against your head, mid back, and tailbone, to force yourself to move from the hip and not the spine. Extend your free leg behind you to help counterbalance your body.

- Push the pelvis forward to help activate the glute as you return to a standing position.

- Do 20 reps on each side.

FOCUS ON FORM
This is a critical foundational movement to master before trying to move on to weighted deadlifts later on.

TIPS

Maintain equal pressure across the ball of your foot to improve your stance control.

Ensure that the low back does not round (which will cause your tailbone to pull away from the dowel) or that the back does not arch (which will cause the mid back to pull away from the tailbone) as you move.

KNEELING BANDED DEADLIFT

■ Securely attach a Powerband to a rack several inches off the ground and step inside, facing away from the anchor point.

■ Position the band at your waist and kneel on a pad positioned far enough away that you feel a fair amount of tension pulling your hips back toward the anchor point.

■ Allow the band to bend you at your hips and sink back toward your heels, then push your hips forward into the band until your hips move into extension. Do not arch your back.

■ Do 50 reps.

TIPS

If you do not have a Powerband, a mountain bike inner tube is a good substitute.

If you feel your back arching at the top of the movement, drop the ribs down in front to put your spine in neutral.

BAND DRIVE THRU

- Securely attach a Powerband to a rack at knee height and step in with one leg, facing away from the anchor point.

- Position the band at the top of your thigh close to your hip crease. Stand on that leg and allow the band to pull your hips back as your trunk hinges forward. Hinge from the hips, not the low back. Keep your knee softly bent.

- Push your hips forward and into the resistance of the band and use your glutes to quickly drive the knee of the opposite leg forward, simultaneously driving the torso upward. Return your foot to floor; that's one rep.

- Do 15 reps on each leg.

TiP

Avoid arching your back at the top of the movement. The goal is to push the hips through while keeping the spine stable.

BANDED HIP DRAG

- Securely attach a Powerband to a rack at knee height and step in with one leg, facing the anchor point. Position the band behind your knee and stand far enough away to feel some tension when your knee is slightly bent.

- Using your glutes, extend your hip behind you. The amount of tension should create resistance, but still allow you to move the thigh behind your body.

- It is critical that you drag your foot along the floor to target the glutes; if you raise your foot you'll recruit the hamstrings. Keep the glutes engaged as you let the band pull your leg forward.

- Do 15 reps on each side.

SLING BACK LUNGE

- Place your foot into a sling at about knee height, shoe laces facing down, and balance on the other leg, with the sling behind you. Clasp your hands in front of your chest.

- Bend your supporting knee to drop into a backward lunge, keeping the shin on the forward leg as vertical as possible. Maintain a neutral spine so that your hip extends behind you, but your back stays quiet.

- Drive back up to the starting position by drawing your legs together.

- Do 2 sets of 10 reps on each side.

TIP
If you don't have a sling, you can also use a box or a chair for this exercise.

SLING PISTOL SQUAT

- Hold the handles of a sling at about chest height with both hands and stand on one leg.

- Extend the other leg straight out in front of you as you squat, keeping the pelvis completely level. Be sure to maintain a vertical shin as you squat down and back up.

- Do 2 sets of 10 reps on each side.

TIP

Stand farther away from the anchor point to make the movement easier and closer to it to make it more challenging.

BANDED HIP JACKS

- Place one TheraBand loop around your knees and another around your ankles.

- Stand on one leg with neutral posture (with even weight distribution through your midfoot), making sure to drive the big toe down to the floor. Place your hands on your hips to feel for any tipping in the pelvis.

- While maintaining stability on one leg, move the other leg out and back at a 45-degree angle from your body. The motion is continuous, not a static hold. Move the hip only as far as you can with zero motion in the pelvis. As you become more stable, aim to move the leg farther.

- Do this for 30 seconds.

TIP

Imagine you have a full glass of water on each shoulder and you want to avoid tipping or moving from the spine or pelvis so you don't spill a drop.

- Repeat this movement for 30 seconds on the opposite leg.

- Keep the bands in place and return to the start position with your hands by your sides. Do 10 jumping jacks. That's one full round.

- Continue this sequence for 3 rounds: 30 seconds of movement on the right leg, 30 seconds on the left leg, and 10 jumping jacks.

SLING ABDUCTOR

- Lie on your side and place your lower leg in a sling so that it sits just below your knee. Clasp your hands together and extend your arms straight in front of you.

- Press down into the sling to raise your hips up while keeping your spine stable. Use your shoulder as your pivot point and stay straight through your torso.

- Do 2 sets of 10 reps on each side.

TIP

To make this easier, move the sling up toward your hip. For more difficulty, move the band toward your ankle.

SLING ADDUCTOR

- Lie on your side and place your upper leg in a sling. Clasp your hands together and extend your arms straight out in front of you.

- Press down into the sling to raise your hips up while keeping your spine stable.

- Do 2 sets of 10 reps on each side.

Alignment Is Not One-Size-Fits-All

The quest for performance in sport leads to the assumption that there is a "best" way. When it comes to running form, if Athlete X performs exceptionally well, it's taken as evidence that X's way is the best way. So the coaching world tells everyone to replicate Athlete X's mechanics. Round and square pegs alike are forced into the same round hole, even though there is a considerable amount of variability among people. Most all of us have experienced the well-intentioned guidance of a coach or teacher as they cram your body into its "best" position. "Run with your feet pointed straight!" the coach tells the kid who runs by duck-footed. "Come to the front of the mat and point your feet straight ahead," the yoga instructor says in a soft, soothing voice. "Keep your feet straight when you squat!" the CrossFit® coach yells as the athletes set up at the weight rack.

But how can someone tell you how to align your body if they don't know your specific alignment? It's impossible to cue alignment without taking into account the idiosyncrasies of an individual athlete's body.

Think about how a door works. You pull on the doorknob, and the door swings open around the axis of its hinge. You can open and shut the door hundreds, thousands, millions of times. All is well. But what would happen if you didn't pull the handle, but instead tried to twist the bottom of the door out to open the door? Well, the twisting would apply a different force through the door, and over time the leverage would either warp the door, break the hinge, or crack the door frame. Trying to make something move in a way it's not designed to move will ultimately break it. When it comes time to question how your feet and hips should be aligned when running, remember: Assess, don't guess.

I cannot count the number of patients I've seen during my career who have had injuries because someone tried to force them to point their legs straight. Just as people have variability in eye color and shoe size, there is biomechanical variability, too. We don't all move through the same axis of motion. Let's stop this madness. Instead of looking for the one way runners should position their legs, let's assess how you are designed so we can help you figure out how you should move.

The position of your bones is not a result of muscle tightness or weakness. And it's not something you can "stretch" to fix. Some people were born with their bones in a certain position,

and some played sports that involved a lot of twisting in their formative years. There is even suspicion that spending a lot of time sitting on your knees with your feet in the "W" position may play a role, but none of that matters now. Your bones are set.

If you don't like the rotational alignment of your bones, you could break your leg and twist it back nice and straight. Clearly, that's a terrible idea! But here's my point: Someone whose body alignment is 100 percent straight isn't necessarily better or worse off than someone who has some twist in their bones. It's just how it is. It only becomes a problem if you don't respect your body.

OWN YOUR MOVEMENT

To figure out how you need to align your body when you move, we have to look at the rotational alignment of your bones, specifically your hips and shins. Imagine that you have a kebab skewer running lengthwise through your leg. Let's figure out how your thighs and shins are positioned on that skewer.

Alignment starts at the hip. Your femur connects to your pelvis at a certain angle. This angle can be described as neutral (oriented straight ahead), ante-verted (twisted inward), or retro-verted (twisted out). The rotation of your hips always dictates where your knees will track, regardless of what we see going on further down the leg. Once we know how your hip is aligned, we can look at the twist of your shin. Just like the hip above, the shin can be straight, twisted inward, or twisted outward. Taken together, your hip and shin position determine how your feet should be positioned.

So how does this play out? Susan and Megan are collegiate runners, and they also do yoga together a few days a week. Both their running coach and their yoga instructor tell them to "point their feet straight." Susan does just that and her body feels great, but Megan experiences knee pain during her runs and in yoga class. We have the runners stand in front of a mirror to watch the way they move.

Susan notices that her thighs and feet are pretty much pointing straight ahead. She squats halfway on both legs and sees that her knees are tracking straight ahead. Next, she stands on one leg and performs a small squat to replicate the amount of bend in her knee as she runs. Once again, her knee tracks straight ahead. Spoiler alert: Susan has a neutral hip and shin alignment, and her natural movement respects her joint alignment—which is to say that she moves the way she is supposed to move.

Megan looks in the mirror and sees her feet pointing straight and her thighs pointing straight as well. But when she squats with both legs, her knees collapse inward. Next she performs a single-leg squat, just like Susan, and again notices her knee collapsing inward. Megan feels really frustrated. She has been doing hip-strengthening exercises to help her knees track straight and feel better, but they obviously aren't working and she's still in pain.

Megan has a neutral hip position like Susan, but her shins twist outward about 15 degrees. If she moves naturally and respects her alignment, her knee will track straight ahead, but her feet will point outward. It's nowhere near the foot position of a Flintstone character, but instead of her feet pointing straight to 12 o'clock, they naturally want to point toward 11 and 1 on the clock face. We tell Megan that she needs to let her feet point out. This feels really weird after an entire running career of being told—and trying—to point her feet straight ahead. She squats down. Her knees track straight. She stands on one leg and squats down. Again, her knee tracks straight. And nothing hurts. Megan flashes a big smile.

When we see a runner wobble or move differently, we often jump to the conclusion that they must have a mobility or stability problem. However, this isn't always the case. Megan's knees weren't collapsing as a result of tightness or weakness—it was a result of over-riding her natural alignment. She needs to respect her alignment in everything she does: running, practicing yoga poses, doing single-leg stability work, and strength and plyometric work. Every time Megan hears the cue "point your feet straight," she now knows to aim her feet for 11 and 1 on the clockface. You'll be amazed at how much more efficient your body can move, and how much less stress your joints will see, when you let them move as they were designed to move.

ASSESS, DON'T GUESS

Assessing the rotational alignment, or twist, of the leg bones is a basic test that physicians and physical therapists learn early on in training. A long time ago, a doctor named Craig realized the importance of rotational alignment. He developed a testing protocol and named it after himself. In recent years, I modified this test to make a DIY version, and many athletes have used it to successfully assess their alignment. If you don't have confidence in your ability to find these landmarks on your own, go see a clinician you trust. But you should try this test first: You'll get critical information about exactly how your body should move during running, and all other sports.

Pinpoint Your Trochanter

Your greater trochanter is a landmark on the side of your hip bone. It sticks straight out laterally. Take a look at the illustration so you know what it might feel like. When we tell people to put their hands on their hips, most people actually wind up putting their hands on the ridge that runs on top the pelvis from front to back (the pelvic crest). Here's what you'll do to ensure you are on the correct landmark on the hip bone (femur).

■ Stand in neutral position, being sure equal weight is on both legs. Place one hand up on your pelvic crest.

■ Now spin your middle finger straight down to the lateral midline of your thigh.

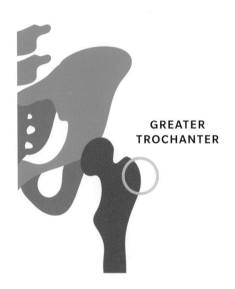

GREATER TROCHANTER

■ As your finger feels the outside of your hip, twist your hip in and out as if it is on a skewer. There's a good chance that you will feel a hard piece of bone in your hip moving beneath your fingers. Congrats. This is your trochanter.

Check Your Alignment

Now we will work with your trochanter to find out the rotational alignment of your hips.

- Stand up and find your left trochanter again (as described on p. 124).

- Keep your hand directly on the side of your hip, and twist the leg inward. The tip of the trochanter will move forward of your hand.

- Then twist the hip back externally and you'll feel the trochanter move back toward your fingers and then past them.

- Continue to rotate the hip in and out until you feel the point in the movement where your trochanter is pointed out laterally.

- Once you have your trochanter in the right spot, hold your leg in this position, and stand with equal weight on both feet. (Don't worry—it's normal to shift away from the hip you were moving to make it easier to do the test.) Let's take a look at your left leg:

If your foot points straight		Your feet should always point straight.
If your foot points in or out		That means your bones have some torsion—either in your hips or your shins. There is nothing wrong here; it's just part of who you are.

- Next we want to identify the path where your knee should track. As naturally as possible, do a small squat, and watch where your kneecap points.

If your knee points straight ahead as you squat		Then it should do the same as you run, bike, etc.
If your knee points outward or inward		You've got some torsion in your hips that you need to respect.

All you have to do now is look at Table 8.1 to see how you should move. Match both your foot position and the direction that your kneecaps point to find out if your bones are neutrally aligned, or if you've got some twist in your hips or shins that you need to respect. Here's one example. Let's say you found out that your knees point out and your feet point straight—this means that you have hips that are twisted out, and shins that are twisted in. You can listen to the coach telling you to "point your feet straight" because based on your alignment that's what they should do. Just be aware that any time you squat doing work in the gym, ride a bike, or run, your knees will shift out more than average. If someone told you to keep your knees tracking straight over your second toe, that would be problematic because your body doesn't move this way.

Knowing what proper alignment looks like for you is really important. When you begin doing strength work in the Running Rewired workouts, make sure you set yourself up according to what you discovered in the trochanter test. When running, make sure you run in a way that respects your body. So many problems can be solved with this one powerful nugget of knowledge.

TABLE 8.1 What Alignment Looks Like for You

	Hips Out	Hips Neutral	Hips In
Shins Out			
Shins Neutral			
Shins In			

Build Better Parts

I want to help you build a better body for better running. To make this happen, we need to optimize the neuromuscular strategy and skills that we use to run. But all of those skills hinge on your ability to show up with robust body parts that are ready to deal with the cumulative load of training. In the same way that a building needs a solid foundation, the structural integrity of your body matters. A lot.

Have you ever been injured from running? It's an indication that the structural integrity of your body parts is compromised! Fortunately, it's not as if all the parts under your skin fail at once. Those individual parts—your bones, muscles, tendons, and cartilage—are all very important, but also very different. And the cool thing about your body is that each of your body parts is optimized for a very specific job.

If you were to ask a typical runner why running is good for them, they might say that running is a great way to develop fitness and build a strong body. If you asked the same question of any biomechanics nerd or knowledgeable physio, they would definitely say that running is a great way to build fitness, but they would stop short of telling you that running builds a strong body. If you truly want to optimize your bones, muscles, tendons, and cartilage, running is not at the top of the list. Actually, for most of these parts, running is close to the bottom of the list. **Simply put, running is not the best strategy to optimize the health of each body part.**

Sure, I see your face turning red with anger. "Hold on," you say. Remember, I'm on *your* side—I want you to keep running and keep crushing it! And that's why I'm giving you the straight-up truth. By now, you know that you need to invest time to develop the skills that will improve your body movement and running. Just stacking up volume won't work. The same goes for your individual body parts. They need individual care, and if you don't approach your training this way, there will be consequences.

INJURIES HAPPEN

You don't have to be a physical therapist to know that *a lot* of runners get hurt. Many runners and coaches are quick to brush this off, saying ,"Well, you did too much, too fast, too soon" (TMTFTS). Indeed, the physical therapy industry can credit 12-week Couch-to-Marathon Training Programs as its single-greatest source of referrals. It's just a bad idea, made even more obvious in hindsight. But it doesn't end there. There's the high schooler who ran a couple of times each week at a casual pace all summer. Fall marks the start of their cross-country season and their training volume and intensity instantly ramps up to four times as much. Boom goes the dynamite; now they are injured. Or maybe it's even more subtle. You've been consistently training 40 miles per week until a fast runner joins your training crew, changing up the dynamic. Pacing ratchets up by 15 percent across the board. The runner's body gets pushed and pushed . . . until it breaks.

Every one of us has been guilty of pushing TMTFTS—yes, even me. But here's the thing, this is not the only road to injury. For every runner I've treated who is prone to bad decisions, I've had a runner who makes excellent decisions and *still* gets hurt. Even though their volume or intensity may not have gone "too far," the cumulative load on the tissue was too much. Again, running isn't conducive to the long-term health of your tissue. Over the past decade, we've learned a lot from studies on tissue morphology, and there are specific strategies that are proven to optimize your body parts for success.

A PLAN TO AVOID INJURY

It drives me crazy when I'm asked, "What's the best exercise for runners?" Or, "What's the best exercise for my hips?" Over my career I've fielded a million questions like this. But this is not what you should be asking. Here are better questions, that deliver actionable solutions:

- How can I optimize my bone density to minimize the risk stress fracture?
- How can I develop strong tendons that won't flare up, especially as I age?
- How can I maintain healthy joints for the long-term?
- How can I maintain muscular strength and power as a runner?
- How can build strength and support in my feet to minimize load on my plantar facia?
- How can I stabilize my hip to keep my partially frayed labrum happy while I continue running?
- How can I build a plan to strengthen my core for running and get rid of my lower back pain?

You get the point. Specific questions deliver specific solutions. This is why click-bait articles offering "3 exercises every runner must do" are so frustrating. If it really was that easy, then runners would stop getting hurt. Unfortunately, it's impossible to "bullet-proof" your body. When you are training on the razor edge day after day, your body parts are incredibly stressed! And it's easy to fall off that edge of safety. Do nothing and you'll become a statistic like most other runners. But if you are willing to put in some effort, we can build guiderails to minimize your risk of falling off that razor edge.

Building a robust body is no different from your physiological training. Does your coach only give you three running workouts and instruct you to hit repeat to PR? No way! Getting fit requires a well-rounded scientific approach to conditioning that matches the demands of the event you are training for. The Running Rewired program is focused on developing the skills that you need as a runner and the parts that support them.

Your body adapts to the load it sees

Training breaks your body down, and after your workouts your body builds back stronger. It's a constant cycle of beat down and repair. Sleep and nutrition are incredibly important to proper recovery, and workout recovery has a role to play as well. With that said, don't get these cycles of work and recovery confused with rest. **Rest doesn't make you stronger.**

To become stronger, your tissues need input. It's a process that is referred to as Wolf's Law—tissues adapt to the stress they see. And this input needs to continue over the long game. Rest provides *zero* input. Still, when runners have pain they are told to rest. Rest will not provide any beneficial input to optimize the tissue at fault. Stew on that as you think about how you are taking a proactive role in your selfcare as an athlete. Don't worry—you aren't alone if rest has been your go-to treatment for all your aches and pains. But do take notice if you have been riding the roller coaster of running-injury-rest-running-injury-rest for way too long.

Too much load can kill

Returning to Wolf's Law, we know tissues adapt to the load they are given. If you hop into your car to go to the track, you don't accelerate to 100 mph right out the driveway. That would be totally irresponsible and negligent. Instead, you take note of kids playing in the street, increase your speed under control through the neighborhood, and then, when you are ready to merge on to the freeway, you make sure it's safe to open up the throttle to match the speed of traffic. Speed and effort need to be progressive. Likewise, as runners, we shouldn't train wide-open, full throttle every day.

Too much load can overwhelm tissues and break them down because they can't repair fast enough. We need to be progressive about how we load the body. The rate of progression and how you monitor it is incredibly important. This is how you know when to safely kick things up, hold steady, or take them down a few notches. In this chapter we will define the optimal dose of input for each tissue starting from where you are now, and taking into account where you are headed. And to do that we need to get into specifics of how each tissue adapts.

BONE IS YOUR FOUNDATION

The most structural aspect of your body is the very bones that give us, well, structure! While we think of them as these solid blocks of mass,

there are two characteristics that need to shape our understanding.

1. Bones are in a constant state of turnover, breaking down and rebuilding.
2. Bones move. Just as your muscles and tendons elongate and rebound, your bones bend and twist.

FIGURE 9.1 Bones Move
Bones are strong but not stagnant. When you load your bones, one side compresses, the opposite elongates, and they twist along a central axis.

This bone movement creates piezoelectrical charges that signal your bone cells to get busy and keep your skeleton healthy to support you in your running. When this breakdown-and-rebuild process is compromised, your bones can break. And when the process is done right, you can build bone better. As a runner, you likely think that all your miles cue your body to build strong bones. The truth is, your bones think running is pretty boring.

We've all been told high-impact activities like running are a great way to maintain and build bone, but research has struck down this lore faster than Usain Bolt can run 100 meters. While your body sees forces as high as 2.5 times your body weight, these forces are not the right type to maintain the health of your bones when running. The force occurs during a specific "time on ground," with every stride you take. As a distance runner, your stance times are generally between 0.17–0.3 seconds with each stride. However, the combination of these forces and the relatively long stance time is not enough to cue your bones to build stronger. In fact, running isn't that much better than sports like swimming and cycling, which are classified as non-weightbearing.

What breaks bone?

Walking into a physician's office and being told you have a stress fracture is one of the worst experiences ever. But I like to rephrase this as: "Congrats. The decisions you made as a runner were so bad, that you broke a bone." It sounds harsh, but it's the truth. There's a lot to unpack here with respect to nutrition and the physics of bone remodeling, so let's dig in.

There are two main types of stress fractures: compressive and tensile. M&M's are a good model for bones, with their hard outer shell and a yummy, chocolate inside. As far as candy goes, they are pretty durable. The inside of your bones is the real deal (the chocolate!) where all

the circulation and metabolism occur. That outer candy shell is like the armor to protect it, just as the outer cortex of your bones protects all the activity going on inside.

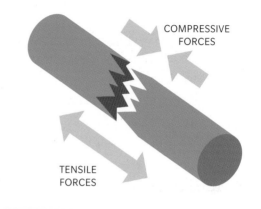

COMPRESSIVE FORCES

TENSILE FORCES

FIGURE 9.2 Bone Forces
Compressive forces drive the bone toward itself. Tensile forces yank the bone apart. Healthy bone can deal with these forces and keep them in check. But when out of balance, they can overload the bone and create a stress fracture.

When most of us think about breaking a bone, we think about short-duration, high-energy events, like getting hit by a bus. Stress fractures aren't quite the same. They occur when things are out of balance from lower-energy loads (much lower than a bus hitting you) and applied for a long time. It is possible to break the candy either by smashing it, or by cracking the candy coating off. Remember bones aren't static—there's a slight bend and twist that occurs when they are loaded. If the bone is strong, the outer cortex withstands all the impact stride after stride. If the cortex is strong enough, it won't crack open, and you won't get a **compressive stress fracture**.

In the other scenario, your muscles and tendons are yanking on the places where they insert onto the bone. That's right, your muscles and tendons load the bone by trying to bow, yank, and twist it. If the bone is healthy enough to withstand all this yanking, you won't develop a tensile stress fracture. However, you are not yet in the clear.

There are two different problems that can happen to throw off this balance. Sometimes, there's a biomechanical problem going on. You may be running in a way that puts too much compression load on a specific part of a bone and it cracks. Or you may have instability in your body such that the yank of the muscles pulls too hard or at the wrong time, and those high tensile loads crack the bone. Improving your biomechanics is an essential step in normalizing those loads so that the problem causing this force overload can be addressed.

Other times, the reason for degraded bone health is completely unrelated to biomechanics. It's actually more of a central or medical issue. Instead of strong bones, good nutrition, adequate energy intake, and normal hormone function (which we call homeostasis), your bones are structurally weak, your nutrition and energy intake are deficient, and your hormonal system is unable to keep things in check and the system malfunctions. To build better bone and repair the system, you will need to do two things:

1. Improve biomechanics of your bone: The workouts in this book will help balance the loads in your bones by getting you to move better, and the plyometric plan will improve the structural integrity of your bones.

2. Keep your nutritional health in check: It's your job to ensure you are taking in enough calories to replace what you are burning. Even deficits in energy intake as small as 350 calories per day can add up over time and ultimately lead to a stress fracture. If you understand what constitutes a healthy diet and know the warning signs, your daily nutrition can contribute to better bone health.

A recipe for better bone

Research shows that people with a history of ball sports are much more resilient to developing stress fractures, facing 60–80 percent less risk than the typical runner! Why? Ball sports require lots of cutting, acceleration, and deceleration. They require fast movement. So the bones see extremely high loads, closer to 3–5 times body weight, coming from multiple directions, and—*this is key*—incredibly short stance times. Tissues adapt to the loads they see, and this force is enough to maintain and build bone. This is why I tell a lot of runners—particularly young runners—that the best thing for bone health is to play soccer, basketball, or ultimate frisbee. Admittedly, this might be a stretch, as many people have limited time. Looking at the research, we can use plyometrics to generate higher forces in a shorter period of time, by following this recipe to build better bone:

Force: Target loads greater than 3.5x body weight, applied for less than 0.1 second.

Movement: Multi-direction is best, but start with mostly vertical jumps while learning proper form.

Dosage: 40 jumps will stimulate your bones. The positive stimulation wears off over the next 4 hours or so. In theory, you could do another set of 40 jumps after 4 hours.

Timing: Do plyo jumps *before* you run. Even a short running warm-up of a few minutes will suppress the bone stimulation effect.

There are a few critical points that bear repeating. And by critical, I mean 100 percent make-or-break. Your time on the ground needs to be *very*, *very* short. It may be the case that you have done plyometrics in the past and understand proper form. If not, in Chapter 11 we'll go into more details on correct plyometric form, but I want this cue to be front and center every time you do plyos: *Get off the ground as quickly as you can.* Please review the additional plyo tips as well. Again, if you spend too much time on the ground, it won't be a stimulus to rebuild bone.

What you need to know about nutrition, diet, and REDs

The team bus can't get your team to the meet on an empty tank. Likewise, your body can't run and train unless you are adequately fueled. It's easy to understand that you need fuel to get through a workout. You may take a pre-run gel or bar to get a boost of calories for a workout. But remember, every time you train you are breaking your body down. In other words, you are literally damaging the structural integrity of your muscles, bones, and tendons. To rebuild those parts you need—you guessed it—fuel! You need to ensure you are consistently taking in enough calories to repair the stress your body gets from training. A large part of this is developing a healthy relationship with food. Nutrition science is an entire book itself, but here's what you really need to know.

TOTAL CALORIES CONTROL ENERGY BALANCE

When it comes to your body weight, research has shown time and again that total calories matter most. Sure, the timing of what you eat, and exactly what you eat may account for 0.1–1 percent of your weight loss, maintenance, or weight gain. But in the end, you either top off the fuel tank for your next mission, or you don't. If you regularly feel like you are starving, you are in a state of low energy availability (LEA) and need more calories to replenish the energy you are using during your workouts or the energy you are using to repair your body.

If this calorie imbalance becomes prolonged, you can develop Relative Energy Deficiency Syndrome, or REDs, which indicates you are lacking the calories required to repair your body. Your endocrine system (i.e., hormones) gets out of whack and your body has trouble keeping its repair process in balance. Your body parts get weaker, and your risk of stress fracture goes up significantly. Sometimes, this is a minor problem requiring a small adjustment. During the season, you may realize you are hungry more often and decide to have a gel or bar prior to your workouts, and this may be enough to fill the calorie void. It's not always so easy.

A 2023 position paper from the International Olympic Committee (IOC) highlights some key findings from recent research on the topic of nutrition. In the past 5–10 years there's been push-back from a lot of people on the role of carbohydrates, particularly as a growing number of athletes have adopted a carbohydrate-restricted diet. It's a loaded topic, and I want to make a clear distinction between the nutrition influencers on social media and independent experts on this panel who study the field intently. To summarize the IOC's position, short-term carbohydrate restriction can compromise strength, power, endurance, cognition, motivation, and recovery. That doesn't sound like the needle is moving in the right direction. In the long-term, carbohydrate restriction can create *"long-term health and performance problems."* In my own experience with athletes, I've seen a lack of fuel cause a major endocrine imbalance that leads to one, two, three, even *four stress fractures in a row*. Getting your first stress fracture doesn't mean you need to freak out. Mistakes happen. But if you are a repeat stress-fracture offender, it's a big red flag that your nutrition, energy balance, and hormonal system are completely out of whack.

The damage created by energy imbalances is not temporary. For female athletes, approximately 90 percent of bone density is established by age 18. For male athletes it's set at 20 years of age. I've worked with elites who had eating disorders when they were younger and they paid the price over their entire professional career.

Be smart. Recognize red flags, such as a negative relationship with food, trouble maintaining your weight, chronic injury, or for women, menstrual cycle irregularities, as they may be warnings that your body needs some extra insight. These red flags won't just go away—you need to take *action*.

Discussing food shouldn't be taboo. Talk to your primary care physician and ask about getting screened by an endocrinologist and/or nutritionist to ensure your body and your food intake are in balance. You need to develop nutritional skills just like you need to develop athletic skills. Seek guidance for issues like this and make it a priority to establish good habits for lifelong health.

QUALITY CALORIES PROVIDE NUTRIENTS

While total calories has the biggest bearing on maintaining your weight, the quality of what you eat does matter. You can eat well as a carnivore or vegan. You can also eat poorly as a carnivore or vegan. The phrase "eat your colors" applies to everyone because colorful foods have a greater variety of vitamins and minerals.

In terms of macronutrients, roughly 20–25 percent of your calories as an athlete should come from protein. If you want hard numbers, as a runner you are looking for 1.2–1.6 grams of protein per kilogram of body weight. Carbs make up the bulk of what you'll burn for energy. And don't be afraid of consuming fat! It is essential for general health as well as a good energy source.

While energy bars are quick and easy, real food packs in more nutrients. If you have questions, look for a sports dietitian in your area. Talk to your coach or a family doctor for some recommendations near you. Maintaining a healthy diet is critical. Failure to fuel your body properly can create lifelong issues.

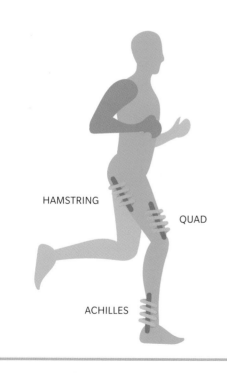

FIGURE 9.3 Tendons Are Springs
While every muscle in your body has a tendon at each end that needs care, the big 3 for runners are the hamstring, quad, and achilles tendons.

TENDONS ARE YOUR SPRINGS

While running, most of us conjure up a visual of our muscles working hard. And of course they are! But we forget about the tendon connecting our muscles to our bones, and how hard they are working, too. Remember, optimizing the elastic energy storage and release in the big rubber bands that are our tendons plays a major role in running economy.

These rubber bands see *a lot* of load. Some of the shorter tendons in your hips may see 1–2 times body weight loads. The patellar tendon sees approximately 3.5 times body weight, and the longer tendons in your lower leg (i.e., your achilles) see 5–7 times your body weight! Tendons have two unique properties compared to other tissues in our body with respect to how they store load and repair.

Loading with viscoelasticity

Basically, the quicker you load your tendons, the quicker they spring back. If you were to interview a muscle, "Hello, Michelle Muscle. Can you describe your perfect day for us?" She would say, "Sure, I'd like to do some super easy load all day long, no problem." You see, muscles are metabolically very active—meaning they have good blood flow to deliver nutrition for long-term action. You could tap your fingers for hours on end, and it's really no big deal for your muscles to continuously raise and lower your finger.

Now if you ask Tina Tendon what she prefers to do, she will tell you she loves to bungee jump off a huge bridge once and be done for the day. Tendons don't have great blood supply, but they are really good at storing high loads, and returning that energy once or twice, and then just chilling out the rest of the day.

A different repair process

If you bruise a muscle, it will automatically start to repair. If you get a paper cut, or even break a bone, your body will automatically enter into repair mode. Every tissue in your body, with the exception of your tendons, have a specific chemical floating around them called substance P. (This is not my attempt to be funny—it's actually called that.) When the body is overloaded, substance P is the messenger that comes out waving a white flag of surrender, "Okay, we need help! Please send in the troops!" Just like that, your body enters into an "inflammatory cascade." I know we've been told inflammation is bad, but that's not always the case. Inflammation cues your body to enter self-repair mode, and ultimately facilitates healing.

In other words, running creates micro-stress in your muscles and bones with each stride.

When micro-damage occurs, muscles and bones can call for reinforcements so the little fires don't flare into bigger ones. But because your tendons have no substance P, they can't initiate their own repair mode. Remember, tendons deal with huge loads while running, and they love that. But they don't get to run a few steps and be done. You are asking tendons to load themselves hundreds of thousands of times per week as you run. When they get a little cranky, they can't optimize their function like other tissues in your body, so they rely on a completely different way to repair: *mechanotransduction.*

> Proximally you have big muscles and small tendons. Distally you have small muscles and long tendons.

Turn movement into repair

The science of tendon health has changed a lot over the past decade, and even in recent years. People continue to use the word "tendonitis" even though it's not scientifically possible.

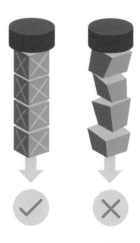

FIGURE 9.4 Tendon Structure Matters
Which one of these structures do you think can better support the loads of running? The intact scaffold or the one breaking down? In *tendinopathy*, the structure degenerates, thus compromising the normal energy storage and release inside the tendon.

The suffix "itis" literally means inflammation of, and by now we know tendons aren't capable of inflammation. When tendons get hurt, **tendinopathy** is a better description of the problem, which is to say that there are degenerative changes inside the tendon. The scaffold that holds the cells together starts to fall apart. And when the structural integrity breaks down, the tendon can't deal with all that elastic energy. You wind up with pain and poor function.

Rest will not make the tendon improve, but it remains the go-to strategy for most runners. They stop running for a few days or even weeks, or they find some other way to cross train for a while. So they have a tendon that is structurally compromised, and by "giving it time," they have provided no positive stimulus to repair or change the situation. And we wonder why tendon pain becomes chronic!

Target tougher tendons

To repair a tendon, we need to load it. Every cell in your body has a wall around it. The novel thing about tendon cells is that they have these little proteins, called integrins, embedded in the walls of the cell. They work like light switches on the wall of the cell. If you rest a tendon, the light switch stays off. But if you start to move and load the tendon, the cellular walls of the tendon will slide against each other. As this happens, they trip the light switches, back and forth. This movement triggers a cascade of actions inside the cell to initiate a repair process that will rebuild the structure of the cell

so it can tolerate the demands of running. The scientific term mechanotransduction literally means "turning movement into repair." The physical tension, compression, and shear on the cells stimulate a chemical repair process to repair the tendon. Don't you feel smarter?

Now you may be thinking "Wait, I'm hurt, and you want me to *move*, not rest? The current research will answer with a resounding "Yes!" But let's be clear about what the research tells us.

BE PROGRESSIVE

As with anything, the load we apply must be gradually progressive. Thus, if your achilles is sore, I would not tell you to do calf raises with 100 pounds on your back. We need to find the right point of entry for your angry tendon. I know the science, but we need to work together to find out where you are currently and how you adapt in order to identify the right amount of load.

Use a 10-point pain scale, where 10 is extreme pain, and 0 is pain free. Research suggests that we aim for 24 reps of load for the tendon, and the effort should not exceed 3–4/10 on the pain scale, either during the exercise or in the 24 hours that follow. If your pain hits 5/10 or more, it doesn't mean that you need to stop exercising, but we many need to lighten the load. Be honest with yourself so we can make a plan and stick with it to ensure that we rebuild your tendon strong!

TOO LIGHT		OPTIMAL DOSE		TOO MUCH LOAD					
1	2	3	4	5	6	7	8	9	10

BE SLOW

The highly viscoelastic nature of tendons tells us they love to be loaded quickly. It won't stress them out, but it also won't speed up the repair process. For optimal results, load the tendon *slowly*. Aim for each of those 24 reps to take 4–6 seconds.

Just like we have a biomechanical recipe for better bones, we have a biomechanical recipe for tougher tendons. It entails slow reps for each main tendon. You have hundreds of tendons in your body, but don't worry—you don't need to do this for each one! We will just tackle the three primary tendons for runners: those in your achilles, quads, hamstrings.

Aim to do these reps at least 2–3 times per week in a progressive format. Again, make your movement slow. These reps can be done before or after your run, or on an off day entirely. I'm also going to ask you to find time to do three additional exercises to load your tendons—calf raises, helicopter lunge, and Swiss curls—at least twice a week.

Tendon Breakdown: Achilles Tendinopathy

Let's apply our knowledge of biomechanics and tendons to an injury that is all-too common for runners: achilles tendinopathy. (Notice I didn't say achilles tendonitis!) Basically, running places lots of load through the tendon with every step, but it's the structure inside the tendon that is breaking down. The tendon can't deal with these high loads and loses its elasticity. To fix it for good you will need to address the biomechanics and rebuild the tendon:

Fix the problem that created the load imbalance in the first place. The job of the achilles is to be a big rubber band to store energy at the start of each stride and release it during the propulsive phase. If that rubber band is on a solid foundation, then it can do its job and you will run pain free.

Achilles issues arise when foot stability is ignored. If there is poor control of the 26 bones inside the foot, the rearfoot (where the achilles inserts) winds up twisted too late in the propulsive phase. With the rearfoot position compromised, the tendon is elongated, thus increasing the mechanical strain inside the tendon and changing the dynamics of the spring. As a result of the higher strain, the tendon gets overloaded and breaks down. So the problem that created the achilles overload isn't the tendon itself, but rather a failure to achieve proper rotational control inside the foot (as discussed in Chapter 6). To address this, first improve the support and control of muscles inside the foot. This will optimize the position of the rearfoot on the forefoot to unload the tendon. Better foot health is integral to the precision workouts in this plan.

Improve the health of the tendon. We know tendons need load, not rest to improve. It's your job to find the appropriate load. To load the achilles tendon, do calf raises. On day 1, you might do 24 calf raises on flat ground, barefoot. Here are some possible scenarios that might play out the next morning and instructions on how to proceed with loading your achilles tendon going forward:

- 1/10 pain level: On the next day, do the calf raises on the MOBO with the fins in the forward slots to take the tissue through a greater range of motion.

- 3/10 pain level: Repeat the exercise barefoot for the next day.

- 5/10 pain level: Your pain level has exceeded what is healthy. Instead of doing nothing, use your opposite (pain-free) leg to provide assistance so that your painful achilles is doing 50 percent less work with each rep.

You can see how the goal is to maintain a beneficial load in your achilles. Use each and every session to keep pushing the needle in the right direction. Afterward, reevaluate and progress the load accordingly until you are consistently moving well without pain. Once you are healthy, further increase load to build durability.

Treat tendinopathy by a) addressing the faulty biomechanics and b) rebuilding the tendon.

CARTILAGE, YOUR GOLDEN SHOCK ABSORBER

How many times have you heard, "Running will wear your joints out?" Well, in this case, reality tells a better story. Cartilage is the incredibly slippery substance that covers and cushions your joints. When it is healthy, your joints feel amazing. And cartilage *loves* compression, decompression, and gliding. It just so happens that this is exactly what running does to cartilage!

Over the past several years epidemiological and imaging studies have proven that people who run minimal to moderate amounts have healthier and more robust cartilage over their joint surfaces as compared to people who don't run. But too much of a good thing can be an issue. There is research to show that groups of people who run in excess of 70 miles per week have a higher risk of cartilage wear. And, yes, I know you read an article about someone running 26 marathons in 26 days. There will always be outliers. That said, the blanket statement that running is going to kill your joints isn't true.

FIGURE 9.5 Cartilage
The incredibly slippery layer of cells that allows your bones to slide freely and smoothly on each other.

Some running is better than not running at all. And more extreme amounts of running have been associated with premature wear. Tell that to your aunt and uncle the next time they haze you for running. But you aren't a research statistic; you are an individual. Find a volume of running that seems sustainable and healthy within the context of your goals.

Take the advice of one of the winningest running coaches of all time, Jack Daniels. If you were to ask Jack, "How far should I run?," he would tell you that it's his goal is to have athletes run the least miles per week that will get the best result. You would think the sport offers a badge of honor to everyone who runs over 120 miles a week—not so. Jack Daniels can show you the training logs of his athletes, who won Olympic and world championship medals by running 35–120 miles a week. Sure, some people rack up more miles, but Jack knows that quality matters more than volume.

LIGAMENTS AND MENISCUS OFFER PASSIVE STABILITY

Both ligaments and meniscus are classified as connective tissues. The job of ligaments is to connect bone to bone. Depending on the position of your joints, your ligaments may be somewhat looser or tighter, but they keep your bones aligned while the muscles and tendons and do the job of moving those bones around. The meniscus is a specific layer of connective tissue inside the knee between the thigh bone and shin bone. It's a shock absorber tasked with improving the congruence of the bony surfaces.

While running on a torn ligament or torn meniscus may in fact be painful, both injuries typically occur as a result of trauma as opposed to the repetitive load of running. Ligaments need a high force acting to tear them. Unless you took a fall and twisted your knee or your ankle (a possible scenario), the act of running forward, up a hill, down a hill, fast, slow, etc., will not tear or compromise your ligaments. Likewise, running alone is unlikely to damage your meniscus. It takes a significant, twisting shear force (e.g., a soccer player cutting hard to one side while wearing cleats) to tear a meniscus.

Muscles pull hard

You can't train your muscles without your nervous system. We know that the nervous system integrates with the appropriate muscle groups to facilitate the skills of running. Chapter 11 will map a plan for how hard and how fast you can train muscle (and your nervous system) to

create more vertical force down to the ground in a shorter period of time to improve your running economy.

I want to leave you with one nugget: If you are looking for gains, *the importance of progressive loading to build muscular strength and power cannot be overstated.* Let's say you are doing quarters on the track and you build up to hit 60-second quarters for eight reps—a challenging workout! However, if you do the exact same workout every week and hit the same splits for each session, however fast those splits are, your body will adapt and plateau. You won't gain fitness without progression. The same thing holds true for your strength and power training. If you can deadlift 200 pounds for 8 reps, that's great. But doing the same thing every session won't get you the progression you are looking for in your running. You should constantly be trying to push the needle toward progress. You may not see all weights for all workouts increase with every session, but when you look back at what you were doing several months ago, you should indeed see progress. Chapter 11 will present a plan to do just this.

FIGURE 9.6 Muscles Pull
You can improve the amount of force and the speed at which your muscles can generate force to maximize durability and performance.

HOW TO MANAGE AGING PARTS

It appears that the search for the fountain of youth is still on. Yes, aging is inevitable. That unstoppable feeling you had when jumping out of bed in your twenties has given way to "Dad noises"—creaks, pops, moans, and groans—as we roll out of bed each morning. Instead of fearing aging, let's take what we know and prepare for it. General studies on aging are conducted on people all over the world, and they provide insight into the strength and mobility issues that occur in the general population. But people who are committed to fitness (yes, I'm talking about you) don't age like the average population. So we need to look at the global physiological changes that occur with aging alongside more specific studies related to aging runners. We can't stop the clock, but we can minimize your losses, and help you have some fun in the process!

Physiological capacity

As we age, our ability to push our hearts and lungs to the max will decrease. You simply will never be as fast at 50 as you could have been at 25, and your VO2max will convince you of that fact. Consistent training can minimize the decline, but it can't swing you back to your prime. Unfortunately, this reality creates systemic ripples in the training of most master runners. Dissatisfied that they can't hit the track splits they threw down in their twenties and thirties, older runners opt to run less hard and *longer*.

Whatever is happening physiologically, your mindset factors into training and performance. All those beat-downs you endured over years of running built up your mental toughness. The stress that used to shock you when you were younger taught you how to maintain a level head under stress and strain. You are able to push through the pain as a result of your hard-earned years of experience. This is why you tell yourself, "I'll just run longer—I'll sign up for an ultra before I embarrass myself at another 5K." It's this attitude that cripples your running program.

No matter what your age and VO2max, there are great health and training benefits from pushing the needle to the redline several times a month. As you look at your weekly training calendar, make time for intensity. Without it, your training will be lacking. Said simply: If you stop running fast, you'll stop running fast!

Mobility

When we are young, our bodies are quite supple. We can easily move our joints through a full range of motion and feel fine when they are fully lengthened under extension or fully compressed into flexion. But as we age, our connective tissues become a bit stiffer and more brittle. Again, some of this is going to occur no matter what, but let's be realistic with that old phrase "Use it or lose it." If you only run, it means that you only take your joints through a pretty small range of motion, so running won't help to keep those joints supple and extensible. For that, you need to take them into and out of end-range positions. You don't need to stretch for an hour a day, or do yoga daily, but you do need to access those positions, and most importantly, stabilize your body in these positions. If you take a look at the exercises in the Running Rewired plan, you'll see we've taken this into account. Move often, move well!

Strength

Study after study shows that people lose muscle mass with age, but this is in *average people*. You don't have to be a research statistic. Most people lose muscle mass with age due to using their muscles less intensely in their day-to-day life and sport. In this chapter, we've learned that tissues need input to adapt and flourish and that running may not be the best way to maintain, let alone increase muscle mass. Let's be totally clear: Running is not a sufficient stimulus to maintain your muscle mass.

Tissues need input, and your muscles require load to adapt. Here's some great news: Strength training can help you maintain, and *even improve your muscle mass*! The legendary Frank Shorter once told me, "It's no secret that I'm not as fast in my 50s and 60s as I was in my 20s. And that can be a bit of a blow to the ego, but you know what's great about strength training? I can still see progress! I'm getting stronger each month, and as someone who's chased performance in my career, that feels really great."

Running form

Because our connective tissues get stiff and our muscles get weak, it is no surprise that we see some significant changes in running gait. Optimal running form requires you to drive your muscular force down to the ground to propel yourself up and forward with each step. With less mobility and strength, you can't maintain that force output and something has to give in your form. Older runners experience less speed, a shorter stride length, stiffer knee angles, and large differences in the distribution of propulsive forces that act on their joints.

Let's reverse engineer this: The "typical runner" gets weaker as they age because their parts can't stabilize and produce force fast enough. You could be a typical runner who doesn't make an effort to improve your mobility, strength, and power and suffer the same fate. Or you could take this as a challenge to focus your time and effort on improving your body, and most importantly, your run. Say it with me—there's always a chance to improve.

Muscle & metabolism

Muscle is hungry for energy. The more muscle mass you have, the more you need to feed it. The less muscle mass you have, the less you need to maintain your body weight. A lot of people try to make metabolism taboo, as if there's some type of secret formula at play. It's just not true. Your daily intake needs are based on your resting metabolic rate (the amount of calories your body needs just to lie in bed and do nothing), the amount of calories you burn when you are *not* exercising (walking around, cooking, cleaning, chores, etc.), and exercising. There are some hormonal factors that play a very small impact on your metabolism, but really, it's a matching game. To maintain your current weight, you need things to be in balance.

Habits matter, and we often don't change our habits to match our body. If you allow your muscle mass to decrease as you age, but you continue to eat the same amount of food, you will begin accumulating a surplus of calories each year. It adds up. Please don't take this personally, but it's important to understand the truth on body image and body composition. Now let's get back to the actionable part: With dedicated time for strength work you can maintain your muscle mass and your caloric needs. Muscle mass is the single-biggest driver of your non-exercise energy needs.

We need more mobility, stability, and strength work as we age. Chapter 11 outlines prehab work, as well as precision and performance workouts. The benefits of precision workouts still hold true, but masters runners have to combat the effects of aging. By making time for two days of training each week, including performance workouts, you will be able to see progress.

Take home

Your body parts need input and they respond to load. Load can mean taking your hips into and out of full extension to work on hip mobility. It can mean initially loading the muscle with a light weight, and as you progress you might use a lot of weight if we are talking about muscle strength. And it can also mean loading quickly in terms of bone health and building muscle power. The Running Rewired program outlines the exercises and volume, but it's up to you to keep up the consistency and build progression in your movements.

Prehab Your Parts for Better Runs

Bone	>	40 plyometric jumps Keep time on ground to less than 0.1 second.	At least 3 days a week, done immediately before your run, or more than 4 hours after your last run.
Tendon	>	24 reps of 3 prehab exercises done *slowly* at 4–6 seconds per rep.	2–3 days a week, as fits into your schedule.
Cartilage + Ligaments	>	Improve joint control and stability; stick to progressive increases in run volume.	The precision workouts will improve these tissues.
Muscle	>	Dosage depends on intent, as detailed in the performance workouts.	The precision workouts target stability improvements, while the performance workouts will improve your strength and power.

HELICOPTER LUNGE

- Set up for the lunge by spreading your legs wide from front to back.

- Helicopters take off vertically, so during this movement, it's critical that you keep your trunk fully upright so the load remains on the knee complex. (Leaning forward so that your upper body is taking off like an airplane transfers load away from the knee and towards the hips, which defeats the point of this exercise.)

- Lunge your knee forward, as deep as you can go. Once you are as low as you can go, "push your lead foot away from you."

- Do 24 reps on each leg—break into sets if needed.

TIP

If you have a MOBO place the fins in the REAR slots and position it under your lead leg. This puts your ankle in a plantar-flexed position to minimize the leverage that your calf muscle can contribute, thus more effectively loading your quad tendon and muscle.

SWISS CURLS

- Lie on your back with a Swiss ball under your heels. Lift your hips into a bridge, keeping your spine straight.

- Without changing the position of your hips, bend your knees as you press your hips up.

- At the top of the movement the soles of your shoes will be on the ball and your thighs will remain parallel with your torso. Don't let the hips flex up. If you feel any tightness in your low back, drop your ribs slightly.

- Do 24 reps, taking 5–6 seconds to do each rep.

TIP

If these become easy, you can do them single leg. If you want to try this, use a transition. On day 1 do 20 reps with both legs, and then 4 single-leg reps on each side. For the next session do 19 reps with both legs and then 5 single-leg reps.

CALF RAISE

■ Using a MOBO for this exercise provides two benefits: The slant board gives you more length to load the achilles and calf, and the toe box will cue you to steer your foot straight and prevent your arch from collapsing as you perform the calf raises.

■ Place the fins in the forward (1, 4) slots.

■ Stand on one leg with a soft bend in your knee. Keep that soft bend as you perform your calf raises.

■ Do 25 reps on each leg. Aim for 2–3 seconds up and 2–3 seconds down.

Build a Bigger Spring

When runners tell me they can't jump, I make it my goal to get them bouncing off the ground, and here's why. While running has been described as a series of single-leg squats, no one can repeatedly perform a single-leg squat while supporting 250 percent of their body weight. There must be more to the story. In reality, running is more like a series of single-leg bounces. Squatting and bouncing place completely different demands on your body. A squat is a time-independent task. You start fully upright with the weight on your back, lower it to a certain height, and rise back up. The load is your focus, and the work is 100 percent dependent on muscular contraction. Conversely, the mechanics of the bounce don't fully rely on muscular work; you get a boost from the storage and release of energy in your tendons.

When you run at a steady-state speed, your foot hits the ground in front of your center of mass. From foot contact to midstance (when the foot is directly under your center of mass) you are in an energy storage phase. From midstance through push-off, you release that energy. Under optimal conditions, the stored elasticity in your tendons covers about half of the mechanical cost of running. That leaves the other half of the contribution to active muscle control. So each leg needs to produce muscular contractions equivalent to 125 percent of your body weight for every step of your run. That sounds a little better, but it's still the case that running isn't easy!

The Running Rewired program is designed to wire your body to move with precision from your foot all the way to your head so that your body can tolerate the stress of running and become more durable. This plan also uses resistance exercises and explosive movements to train your body to develop speed. Improving your bounce is best achieved with safe exercises that train movements, not exercises that build up individual muscles. This kind of training will transform your body and running stride in ways you've never felt from running alone. It's where the fun starts and performance barriers come crashing down. Don't worry—this is not CrossFit for runners. That would entail a big dose of exercise volume to condition the body for general fitness. Our goal is to impose a specific stress on your body to produce a specific result that will improve your running, making you faster.

Muscular Endurance Doesn't Equate to Speed

Running applies a stress to improve or at least maintain muscular endurance, which is the ability to apply a given load over and over again for a long time. It stops short of developing the skill of force production for improved speed and running economy. Research shows that strength in distance runners declines with age. So endurance training alone doesn't develop all the skills you need to run. Failing to do anything outside of running eventually leads to a loss of athleticism. The good news? Targeted strength training helps younger runners, middle-aged runners, and older runners improve their running economy. If you need more incentive, an incredible study involving more than 26,000 athletes found that strength training reduced sports injuries by 33 percent and cut overuse injuries in half. Deliberate strength training is well worth your time.

ECONOMY VERSUS PERFORMANCE

We all love being economical. Whether it's your finances, groceries, or running form, it feels good when your choices don't bleed money or effort. And as we've learned, one key to better running is capitalizing on the free storage and release of elastic energy. If you can improve your stride so you're using less muscle energy to run at a given pace, you can hold that pace longer without fatigue or have the energy reserves to run faster at the same effort. But there comes a point where we sacrifice economy for speed: Clearly, the high school kid who wins the stoplight drag race is driving a Mustang, not a Prius. Running is no different; it's speed that wins medals, not economy.

As speed increases, your foot spends less time in contact with the ground. So to run faster, you've got to train your body to deliver force more quickly. If I take an untrained runner into my lab and measure the amount of force he can produce, it will take about half a second for him to hit his max value. It takes time to develop peak force. But you don't have the luxury of being on the ground very long when you are running—in fact, most runners spend only about a quarter of a second (or less)

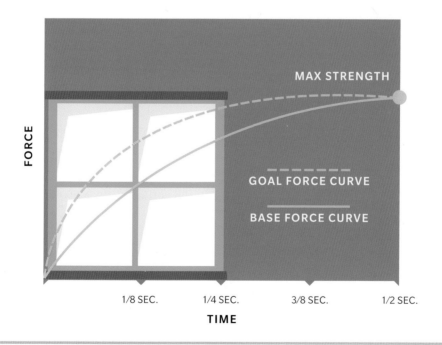

FIGURE 10.1 Force Curve
Max strength isn't the goal. Instead, the focus is on the slope of the curve: the rate of force you generate. Train your body to develop force quicker to improve your run speed.

on the ground, so we need to train our bodies to produce results in this window of opportunity (see Figure 10.1). Research shows that the runners who put more force down to the ground at a faster rate will run faster. Increasing maximum strength at half a second doesn't correspond to run speed. This is the entire premise for an intervention of strength and plyometric training. It sounds promising, but before we get started, let's look at how it works.

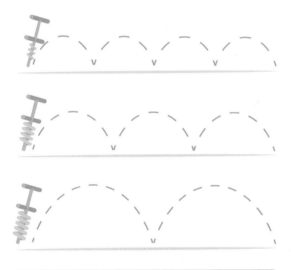

FIGURE 10.2 Running Economy
The pogo stick illustrates how a stiffer spring delivers more force to the ground, which leads to favorable gains in both speed and distance.

BUILD A BIGGER SPRING, GET A BIGGER BOOST

Let's imagine that you come across a pogo stick that belongs to a kid in the neighborhood. It's pretty old, so the spring isn't very stiff, and to be honest, you aren't the 50-pound kid it was designed for. Feeling nostalgic, you pick it up and bounce around, but the pogo stick doesn't rebound very high and you don't cover much ground per hop. So you buy a pogo stick made for adults. It has a much bigger spring, and there's a huge difference in the amount of rebound you can achieve following every hop. It feels a bit awkward, but you can cover more distance per jump than you did on the neighbor kid's pogo stick. After a week of practice you figure out the timing of the energy storage and release in the spring. You discover that if you really jump "into the spring," it launches you back up. Now you are covering more ground per stride than you ever did as a kid.

The distance and speed of your bounce depends on how much load is applied to the ground both in terms of the storage and release in the spring of the pogo stick and the timing of your jump. This is similar to what happens when you do run-specific strength training. By incorporating strength and plyometric work into your training, you build a stiffer spring. This stiffer spring allows you to put more force down to the ground with each stride. And optimizing the timing of your muscular output will yield even more gains. The additional force coming from both your muscles and the loaded spring translates to more hang time, which means you are covering more ground per stride. And that's how you get faster.

more force + higher RFD = running economy

To generate more oomph from your muscles, we need to target your rate of force development (RFD), which is directly correlated to running speed and athletic performance. We'll use a combination of strength and plyometric exercises to build the skill of force development. And that's a key distinction between the Running Rewired plan to improve your running and a plan to improve your calf circumference. Your success in a single exercise isn't the key. The exercises in this chapter are simply a vehicle to teach the skill of force production.

Neurological stiffness is critical to optimize elasticity

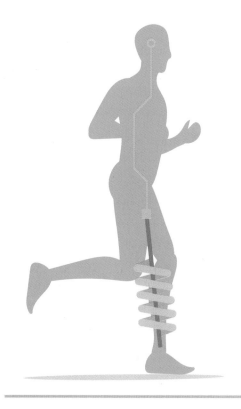

FIGURE 10.3 Intermuscular Coordination and Limb Stiffness
The power to run comes not just from isolated strength, but by the brain learning to stabilize, smooth, and sync muscle control for better elasticity and faster splits.

Work for a Stronger, Longer Stride

If you can increase the amount of force you apply to the ground, you'll cover more distance per stride without even trying. This is the safe way to improve your stride. You could simply force a longer stride length, but that would put excessive stress on your body. Think of it this way. A marathon takes around 20,000 steps. If you can gain 1 or 2 free centimeters per stride, you'll be ahead of where the pre-trained version of yourself would have been at the same step count. And you will finish ahead of your previous PR.

Force production requires both muscular changes and wiring changes. Muscles generate force. After a bunch of strength training in the gym, muscles get stronger and eventually they become a bit bigger and denser as a result of a process called hypertrophy. A larger muscle produces more force per area. This program targets the movements that will improve your muscular force production for running. But we also need to train the brain to effectively train the muscle. Remember that a muscle needs to be told to contract by the nerve to which it is attached. Each muscle fiber connects to a nerve called a motor unit, which coaches the muscle to work efficiently and apply more force. With a little rewiring you will get better at:

Training more muscle fibers (or motor units) to activate at once. Your muscle isn't a monolithic mass, but rather thousands of muscle fibers. If you want to extend your knee straight while sitting, you only need a small percentage of those fibers inside the muscle to fire and lift your leg. To lift 200 pounds off the floor, your body will need to recruit more muscle fibers at once to produce more force.

Delivering the message to the muscle faster. An explosive movement is critical to run-specific training because running requires you to deliver a big force down to the ground in a short period of time. When the nerve communicates faster, the muscle can be fired more quickly.

Muscle coordination and synchronicity. Muscles don't work in isolation. This plan will develop intermuscular coordination to prepare the right muscles to fire together at the right

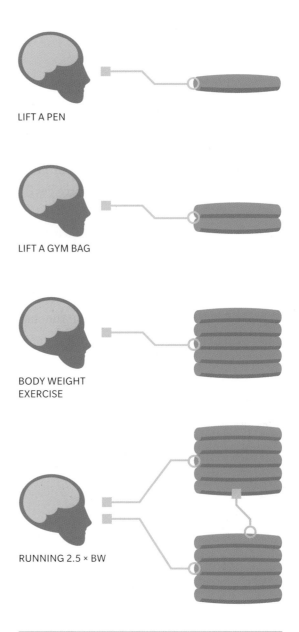

LIFT A PEN

LIFT A GYM BAG

BODY WEIGHT EXERCISE

RUNNING 2.5 × BW

FIGURE 10.4 The Body Responds to Force
The greater the load, the more muscle fibers we wire up and fire up. But body weight exercises alone don't require the force output of running. The Running Rewired performance and power workouts deliver the overload that trains the muscle output to handle the demands of running.

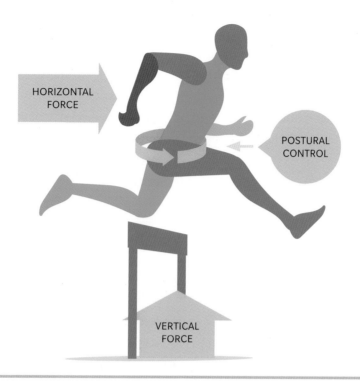

FIGURE 10.5 Running Rewired

The strength and plyometric exercises in this program provide specific gains to meet the demands of running.

time and allow the opposing muscle to dial down so you aren't fighting your movements with excessive co-contraction.

The Running Rewired plan ultimately targets both muscle intelligence and system intelligence so your body can coordinate its movement and you can overhaul your stride.

HOW TO BUILD A STRONGER SPRING

A solid plan to build a better spring doesn't have to be grueling or time-consuming. It also

doesn't have to feature muscle confusion, muscle occlusion, or a host of other trendy terminology. We will use the process of overload of fundamental movements to demand more from your body in a calculated way, and your body will respond.

To achieve run-specific gains, you will need to practice the movements that will achieve these three objectives:

1. Produce horizontal force with a powerful deadlift pattern. This includes front-to-back movements that engage the powerful muscles around the hips.

2. Produce vertical force with a fluid squat pattern. This involves mostly up-and-down movements that split the work between the muscles around the knees and the hips.

3. Establish 3D postural control in the core. Moving heavy loads requires the core to be engaged, anchoring the legs and upper body.

Every movement fits into one of these three categories. And every movement has a specific purpose: to improve your running. Variety and repetition are the building blocks of motor learning and skill development. When you become stronger, your preferred muscle recruitment shifts from the front side of your body to the backside of your body. This allows you to maintain better postural control and put more drive into your gait. Some truly magical things happen to your running form once you change what your body is capable of achieving.

First, Focus on Form

Correct movement starts with your ability to maintain a stable spine while moving into a squat and deadlift pattern. In Chapter 7 we practiced this skill with the chair of death squat (p. 109) and the single-leg deadlift (p. 111), using a dowel to test whether your spine remained in neutral. If your body pulls away from the critical points of contact during the chair of death squats you will not be able to safely generate the vertical force production. Likewise, if your back rounds or your lower back moves away from the dowel during the single-leg deadlift, you will not be able to produce the horizontal force needed for a powerful deadlift. In either case, you'd be better served spending 10 minutes every day for a week nailing these movements with precision. Once you add weight to these movements or attempt to move faster, small details become huge. If you cheat the movement when load is increased, you risk overstressing your body, and the gains we are working toward will not readily transfer into your running! Some runners naturally have body awareness and others don't. Some will progress quickly toward the more complex movements in this plan, and others will need to take a slower approach to the program. Whatever the path, every athlete can improve. If you are struggling with fundamentals, focus on achieving skilled movement, and with consistency you will progress through this program. There's nothing to be gained by mixing poor form with a stack of weights.

Keep in mind that good form requires feedback. Recruit a friend to join you in these workouts so you can help each other on proper movement. Or use your smart phone to record a video and see if your movement follows the exercise cues. Again, form is the key to transferring these skills into your running gait.

How heavy is too heavy?

Intensity is fundamental to these exercises. Go as heavy as you can while retaining perfect form. The goal is to build a resilient movement strategy under stress; that's the skill that will improve your running. As you add load, you'll find the cracks in your movement program. For example, your legs may be able to push a heavy weight, but your core collapses. When you can't stabilize what your legs are driving, you are driving drunk—and that's just not safe! If your back starts to round when you deadlift 150 pounds, master the position with 135 pounds. Remember that your body is adapting many things to allow you to move well under stress.

Use this guideline to decide when you are ready to increase your load: If your form doesn't break down and the speed of your lift doesn't decrease more than 50 percent within the set, add weight.

Some of the lifts have weight targets for you to work toward. These goals are within your reach. I've helped people who have never been in a gym transform into strong runners using these same guidelines. Once you change your recruitment strategy, you'll be shocked at how much better your run feels—and what your body can do if you commit to the effort.

Don't Believe Everything You Hear About Strength Training

Before you get started, there are a few myths about strength training to debunk. The first concerns bar speed. There's a lot of buzz about super slow lifting, or taking 5–10 seconds to press the bar up and the same time to lower it. Slow lifting skills won't transfer to running, so skip it. Keep your bar speed smooth and consistent. When it comes to strength, your lifting and lowering movements shouldn't take longer than about 2.5 seconds total. In fact, if your bar speed slows considerably, your set is over. Admittedly, the last few reps of a set will be more difficult, but we are not lifting to failure (i.e., the point where you literally can't push any more and the bar is creeping along). If the plan tells you to do 6 reps, and you hit 4 reps at a consistent rate of movement, but the final 2 reps are really slow with excessive strain, you need to reduce the weight. Think of it like a track workout. If your goal is to hit 8 quarters in 78 seconds, intervals 7 and 8 still need to be on pace. Choose a challenging weight that allows you to achieve quality reps for the full set.

Plenty of experts claim that you should hold your breath during a lift, but this is bad advice. The theory is that the trapped air adds stability. The core muscles in your back need to fire up to provide the stability that prevents your body from bending under an increased load. Your core will work overtime during heavy lifts, and you can't depend on a bubble of air to keep you in alignment. Plus, you don't hold a stagnant bubble of air in your diaphragm when you run, so don't do it when you lift. If you find that you have to hold your breath for each and every rep, it's a sign that your legs are writing checks your core can't cash, so reduce the amount of weight until you can execute the movement with good form and steady breathing. There is nothing wrong with inhaling on the way down and exhaling on the way up, but just keep the air moving.

$$\frac{(strength + power)}{body\ weight} = performance$$

Finally, there's the common misconception that strength work will cause you to bulk up. The goal is to be as strong and powerful as you can at a given weight. And when it comes to training, building strength and power can be progressed and achieved by training with *intensity*. But when it comes to putting on bulk, it requires a focus on **volume**. Make no mistake, I'm going to ask you to show up to your training with intensity, but the dosage in the Running Rewired program does not entail enough volume to cause you to "bulk up."

Additionally, running burns a lot of calories, and adding significant bulk means you need to have a calorie surplus. Given the demands of training, it's unusual for runners to put on much weight at all, but let's say you do in fact gain a pound on this plan. That pound of total muscle mass will equate to massive improvement in applying force down to the ground. And that increased strength directly impacts stride length.

A bigger spring is better ... and faster.

Get serious, not fancy

Progress in the gym comes from consistency and intensity, not trying every random exercise you find on social media. The specific exercises in this plan were chosen because they are proven to be effective in producing gains in your running, and because they are fairly safe to perform. I've tried to provide enough variety to keep things interesting and solve problems. So before you tell me that you need new exercises to keep from being "bored," dial up the intensity of your performance lifts.

Evolving point of view

When I began lifting weights as a 13-year-old swimmer, my coach was strict on movement and maintaining a neutral spine position. By the time I was studying physical therapy in college, the evidence still reinforced a focus on holding a neutral spine throughout your reps.

In the past few years, studies have emerged showing that people who lift weights with a rounded spine don't necessarily have a higher incidence of low back pain compared to people who lift with a "better" straight spine. So, do I allow my runners to lift with a rounded spine position now? No way!

I'm not in the business of training weight-lifters. I'm in the business of optimizing athletes for the demands of their sport. And one of the key skills in sport is to dissociate movement of the spine from movement of the hips. Why? Because the skill of postural control greatly affects running economy. A focus on neutral spine trains your spine position during your reps and builds better capacity for postural endurance for both short, hard efforts and long runs. As always, research needs to be put into context, because context better guides the specific action you take to achieve your goals.

TRAINING HORIZONTAL FORCE

LANDMINE SINGLE-LEG DEADLIFT

- Position one end of a 45-pound Olympic bar on the floor in the corner to anchor it.

- With the free end of the bar perpendicular to your body, stand on your outside leg and hold the bar in the opposite hand; let your arm hang down straight. Raise your free arm out to the side for balance if needed.

- Hinge your hips back while keeping your spine completely straight and lower the bar while raising your back leg behind you.

- Push your hips forward into the bar to return to the starting position.

- Face the opposite direction to work the other side.

- Do 3 sets of 8 reps on each leg.

TIP
Always look in the same direction as your chest is facing. Moving your head before beginning the bend will bring the spine out of neutral.

ROMANIAN DEADLIFT

- Stand in front of an Olympic bar with your shins touching the bar and feet shoulder-width apart. Squat down and hold the bar with an alternating hand grip. Imagine twisting your arms outward as if snapping the bar in half to lock the shoulder blades back and down along the ribs.

- Keeping a straight spine, drive your hips up into standing position.

- Push your hips back, away from the bar, as you lower it straight down to the floor (or you feel tightness in the hamstrings).

- Push your feet down through the floor to drive your hips forward from the glutes and return to standing position.

- Do 3 sets of 8 reps. The 8-rep goal is 1.5–1.8 times body weight.

TIPS

Make the weight as heavy as possible without rounding your low back.

The bar must track straight up and down as hips move back to front.

Keep your shoulders locked back and down on your ribs through the entire movement to help stabilize the spine.

Your head position is critical for spinal stability. Imagine a camera on your chest pointing forward. Throughout the movement, only look exactly where the camera is filming. If your chest is down, you should be looking down. Don't look up early as you are driving back up.

MODIFIED START POSITION

If you have tight hamstrings, don't attempt to pick up the bar off the floor. Instead start with the bar on a rack or boxes at mid-thigh height. Tight hamstrings will force you into a rounded low back and prevent you from getting into good position. Tightness will also determine the depth of your hip hinge. It's better to have a shallow hinge and preserve perfect postural alignment than to get the bar lower and round the back.

HIP THRUST

- Sit with a weighted Olympic bar across your hips. Use a bar pad or rolled-up exercise mat as a cushion between the bar and your hips.

- Lie back with your head and shoulders on the floor, your hands on the bar several inches out from your hips, and your knees bent.

- Push your hips and bar straight up while maintaining a completely neutral spine.

- The goal is 2 times body weight.

- Do 3 sets of 6 reps.

TIP

Don't go any higher than neutral so that you don't irritate your low back.

KETTLEBELL SWING

- Stand with your feet set slightly wider than shoulder-width apart, and hold a kettlebell in front of you with both hands, arms straight.

- Press your hips back as if you're squatting while leaning your torso forward, allowing the kettlebell to drop down and back between your legs.

- Explode quickly to get the weight to shoulder height—enough that you have to brace the core to "brake" the weight from moving higher.

- As the weight falls back down, hinge backward again at the hips.

- Do 3 sets of 8 reps.

TIPS

You should feel this in your glutes and hamstrings, not your low back.

To increase difficulty, have a friend stand in front of you and push the weight down with each rep.

Choose a weight that you can move quickly.

KETTLEBELL SQUAT

- Hold a kettlebell tight to your chest in both hands with shoulder blades spread wide and locked down on the back. Your feet should be slightly more than shoulder-width apart.

- Staying centered over your feet, sink your hips back and down in a squat until your elbows touch your thighs.

- Keeping neutral spine, drive back up to standing position.

- Do 3 sets of 8 reps.

TIPS

You can also use a dumbbell, sandbag, or any kind of weight for this exercise.

Don't arch your back at the top of the movement to counter the weight. Maintaining a neutral spine through the movement ensures that your core works as much as your legs.

SPLIT SQUAT

- Hold a weight in each hand, arms extended by your sides, and rest the top of one foot behind you on a bench in a staggered stance.

- Let the weights hang straight down as you perform a single-leg squat.

- Aim to keep your trunk as vertical as possible and your shoulders packed down and along your ribs as you move down into the squat and return to standing.

- Do 3 sets of 8 reps.

SQUAT

- Set up the Olympic bar in the rack at approximately the height of your shoulder blades. Walk under it so that the bar is resting just above your shoulder blades and across your traps.

- Focus on breathing 360 degrees around your spine. Imagine you are trying to inhale and expand a belt around your waist. You aren't going to hold the breath, but instead focus on using your breath to provide tension for your spine.

TIPS

The key to maintaining a neutral spine with a squat is your setup. Keep this sequence in mind before each and every set. Proper form at the top of the squat ensures success once you drop down.

Have a training partner assist you with getting the bar on and off your shoulders and spot you if the bar gets too heavy.

- Now stand up straight and step back out of the rack to begin your set.

- Push your hips back to drop into a squat. There is no need to squat past the point where your thighs are parallel to the ground.

- Push your feet through the floor to return to standing.

- Do 3 sets of 6–8 reps. The 6-rep goal is 1.3–1.5 times body weight.

OTHER SQUAT VARIATIONS

Box Squat: Place a bench behind you so that at the bottom of each rep you will briefly make contact. This helps you learn proper squat depth and increases the demand on the backside muscles.

Offset Squat: For a core challenge, place an additional 10 percent of the total weight on one side of the bar. The offset load can help target imbalances. Split your sets to train both sides.

SLING ROW

- Grab the handles of your sling trainer with each hand, and lean backward, making sure to keep your bodyline straight, and elbows fully extended.

- Draw your hands in toward your chest, squeezing the space between the shoulder blades together while keeping the neck and upper traps relaxed.

- Do 2 sets of 10 reps.

ARCHER PRESS BRIDGE

- Set up the sling trainer so that the handle is at chest height. Hold the handle in one hand and a light weight (5–15 lb.) in the other.

- Lower your body into bridge position, bringing the weighted arm parallel to the arm holding the sling.

- Twist your body down and away from the sling as if you are an archer pulling back on a bow.

- Pull yourself up with the hand on the sling so that it twists your body while simultaneously punching the dumbbell forward.

- Do 3 sets of 6 reps on each side.

TIPS

If you feel any tightness in your low back during the movement, drop your hips an inch or two lower.

If you don't have a sling, you can hold on to a bar in a squat rack.

PUSH-UPS

- Place your hands on the floor with your thumbs pointing forward and fingers pointing out to help screw the shoulder blades flat along the back. Start in a high plank position.

- Drop down into a push-up, but don't let your elbows move past the torso. This will keep your shoulders healthy.

- Return to start position.

- Do 3 sets of 10 reps.

TIPS

To make it easier you can switch to your knees.

For an additional challenge, lift one leg slightly off the floor and switch legs halfway through the set.

SLING PUSH-UPS

- Place your hands in the sling and start in plank position, with either one or two feet on the floor.

- Drop down into your push-up, without letting your elbows move past the torso.

- Return to start position.

- Do 3 sets of 10 reps.

TIP

Move your body forward of the attachment point to make the movement easier and straight beneath the attachment point to make it more challenging.

WAITER CARRY

- Hold a kettlebell or dumbbell in one hand and raise your arm so that your upper arm is parallel to the floor, and your forearm is vertical. Allow the weight to slide your shoulder blades back.

- Keep your ribs down in front to avoid arching your low back, and walk around for at least 30 seconds.

- Do 4 reps.

TIP

The goal here is not to go heavy (5–15 lb.), but to build a postural stability by maintaining a shoulder blade that is flat and back along your ribs and a high elbow.

SUITCASE CARRY

- Hold a kettlebell or dumbbell in one hand, and let it hang down at your side.

- Keep your shoulder blades packed down along your ribs and actively counter your tendency to lean away from the asymmetric load.

- Hold yourself completely vertical as you walk for 30 seconds.

- Do four 30-second carries.

FARMER CARRY

- Hold a weight in each hand, allowing them to hang down at your sides while you keep your shoulder blades packed down along your ribs and the back of your neck long.

- Hold this posture as you walk forward for 40 seconds. Take full, natural steps, not short and choppy ones.

- Perform 3 sets.

▷ TRAINING PLYOMETRIC SPEED AND STRENGTH

Some of the movements we do to build a better spring consist of moving less weight (and sometimes only body weight) very fast. Plyometrics are jumping movements that train tendon response to optimize elasticity. To achieve this, your time on the ground has to be very brief. This entails one fluid movement where you explode off the ground like your life depends on it. To facilitate this quickness, I expect you to rest as needed.

The goal specified for the plyometric exercises is the total number of repetitions performed at high intensity. If the exercise specifies 10 reps and you need a break after 3 reps to maintain a high-intensity effort, take 15–20 seconds and then get back at it. If you are new to plyometrics, take a short break after 5 reps of any exercise. Even experienced athletes will need to recognize when to rest. If you notice that you are double bouncing on your landing, you've lost your spring. Double bouncing works the muscle, not the tendon response. Take as much rest as you need to do quality reps with both quickness and high intensity.

When it comes to plyometrics, keep in mind that bigger is not always better. Some of the exercises use a box jump. It looks cool to jump up on a box that's at chest height, but it won't help you run better. Excessively tall box jumps require you to muscle through the jump, which increases your time on the ground. Once again, this means you are no longer training the spring; you are doing nonspecific strength work. The best height for a plyometric exercise is the one that allows you to get off the ground quickly. For most athletes, the jump box should be at mid-shin or knee height (around 14–18 inches).

Only when you can jump higher without compromising the speed of your time on the ground should you use a taller box. Even then, there really isn't much benefit to be found. I've never used a box taller than knee height to train an athlete to increase the rate of force development. Instead of looking for a taller box to jump, aim to get off the ground quicker with each jump. If you don't have access to a jump box, park benches, high curbs, or retaining walls work great.

Strength is a time-independent. Running is a time-dependent.

Technique for Plyometric Exercises

- Form is as important as intensity for plyometric exercise. Practice in front of a mirror to get feedback on your form.

- Don't let your knees collapse in when you land a jump. As for the rest of your leg alignment, it should be exactly what you saw in Chapter 8 (see Table 8.1 on p. 127).

- Keep your hips back on landing. If your knees are roughly over your toes, your hips are where they need to be.

- Land with your full foot. Sure, your forefoot will come down first, but the full foot should make its way down to the ground. This will help get your hips back, and allow you to fire the hip, knee, and ankle muscles together. When all of these joints work together it is called a triple extension, and it's the key to getting mechanics of the movement right. Staying up on your toes lets you cheat and jump only from the calf. For plyometric exercises I use the cue "drive your feet through the floor" to ensure each joint fires correctly as you drive up off the ground.

If you can't land a jump correctly, revisit precision workouts 1, 2, 4, and 6 to clean up these movement imbalances for several sessions and then attempt the plyometric exercises again.

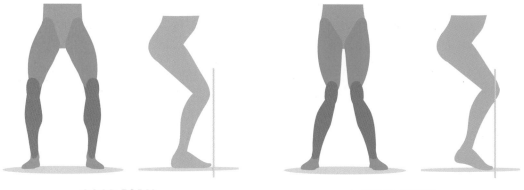

GOOD FORM   POOR FORM

FIGURE 10.6 **What to Watch For**
Notice the position of the knees in the front view and the position of the hips and knees in the profile view.

DUMBBELL PUSH PRESS

■ Start in a split stance with one foot just in front of the other, and hold a dumbbell in each hand positioned just in front of your shoulders.

■ Dip down slightly and explode upward into a jump so that your momentum drives the weights overhead. While you are in midair, drive the forward leg back behind you to land in a switch stance.

■ The goal is to keep the distance between the knees tight, as in running. You don't need to go into a deep lunge.

■ Do 10 reps on each leg.

TIPS

This is not a shoulder exercise. Keep the weight light and the explosive drive high.

If you find yourself landing forward of where you started, place a box in front of your forward foot to force yourself to focus on an upward movement.

This movement at your hip is identical to the banded hip drag exercise (p. 114).

NINJA SQUAT JUMP

- Stand facing a box or bench that is approximately mid-shin height.

- Jump up off both feet and land as softly as possible on top of the box on your full foot (not just the ball of the foot), with your knees bent to about 90 degrees. Stay low and hold for a count of one.

- As you jump back down to the floor, start driving your feet into the floor before you land so that you can immediately drive back up on top of the box.

- Do 20 reps.

TIP

Do not double bounce. If your time on the ground increases, take a break. The goal here is to be elastic!

BOX SQUAT JUMP

- Set up a box or bench that is about mid-shin height and another box or bench about three feet away that is roughly the same height or slightly taller.

- Start from a quiet seated position, and then explode up and forward so that you land on the box in front of you. Stand tall on landing.

- Step (don't jump) back down.

- Do 20 reps.

LATERAL HURDLE HOP

- Place a small hurdle, foam roller, or other object on the ground and hop sideways over it from one foot to the other.

- Continue jumping for 30 seconds. Do 3 sets.

TIP

Keep your hips level at all times—don't allow them to collapse inward.

SPLIT BOX JUMP

- Find a box or bench that is about mid-shin height.

- Place one leg up on the box and explosively drive your body upward, switching your leg position in midair.

- When you get back on the floor, aim to explode up immediately again upon contact. Double bouncing is not allowed!

- Do 30 reps.

TIP

Aim to drive equally through both legs on each jump.

BURPEES

- From a standing position, drop down to the floor in a tuck, and then into the high push-up position with thumbs pointing forward and fingers pointing out.

- Drop into your push-up until your elbows are in line with your torso.

- In one motion push up and tuck your legs under your body, and then explode upward, reaching your arms high. This is one full rep.

- Do 3 sets of 6 reps.

Medball exercises

The medicine ball can be used to learn the skill of force production. It gives you a target to initiate the movement, and the body is pretty good at following. If you concentrate on driving the ball as hard as possible, it will help ensure your legs follow with intense directional force. These exercises are deceptively hard and equally rewarding, and they serve as a great introduction to plyometric training.

MEDBALL PUSH PRESS

- Hold the medicine ball in both hands at chest height.

- Use your legs to drive upward in an explosive movement. Your lower body generates the momentum to drive your arms and the medball overhead.

- Do 25 reps total. Each one should be max intensity with rest as needed.

TIP
This is not a shoulder exercise! Keep the ball weight light (10–20 lb.) and the explosive drive upward high.

MEDBALL GRANNY TOSS

- Hold a medicine ball in both hands.

- Quickly drop both the medball and your hips down and then explode upward, blasting the medball overhead as high as possible. The legs do all the work to accelerate the ball.

- Do 25 reps.

MEDBALL
TWIST 'N' CUT

- Hold a medicine ball with both hands and stand in a slight squat position.

- Quickly wind the ball to one side, and then twist and explode to the opposite side, aiming to throw the ball as far as possible laterally.

- Run over to the ball, pick it up, and repeat the movement, throwing the ball in the opposite direction.

- Perform 20 reps.

MEDBALL
TRIPLE BOUND

- Hold a medicine ball with both hands and lean slightly forward.

- Throw the ball forward as hard as possible while launching yourself into a forward bound, followed by two more bounding jumps for distance. The medball helps initiate a greater horizontal force through the hips.

- Do 5 reps.

MEDBALL ACCELERATION SPRINT

- Hold a medicine ball with both hands and lean slightly forward.

- Throw the ball forward as hard as possible while launching yourself into a full sprint for 20 meters. The medball helps initiate the horizontal force to accelerate.

- Perform 6 reps. Rest 1.5 minutes between each rep.

A Master Plan to Master Running

Building a house requires a plan. Building a syllabus for a college course requires a plan. Building a training calendar to develop your physiological capacity requires a plan. And rewiring your muscle memory and improving your rate of force development requires a plan. The Running Rewired program is a system of workouts designed to bring about specific adaptations in your body to impact your run. Doing random exercises and workouts won't help you target a specific result. Transform your body and run for success with these workouts, which will improve your movement precision and build your spring for better performance.

The movements in this plan are safe. Truth be told, there are even more Olympic lifts that could have been added to the performance workouts, such as cleans and snatches, that are capable of improving running-specific mechanics in amazing ways. But they also require considerable and precise hands-on coaching to get them right. It's not worth spending extra time trying to learn complex exercises when you can nail the fundamentals and get all the benefits. Each movement in the following workouts has a purpose that is keenly focused on your specific needs as a runner. Variety and repetition are the building blocks of motor learning. The Running Rewired plan has enough of both to produce solid results. But it's up to you to add the consistency that will bring results to your running.

The topic of consistency is one that cannot be overstressed. Life happens. Sometimes you get sick, or you are up with a screaming toddler all night. You may deem it a better use of your time to study for your upcoming test rather than head out for a run or a workout. There will be times when workouts and runs get dropped. But the aim is for this to be the exception, not the rule. All is not lost if you skip one gym session four weeks prior to your 10K race, but if you only get in a single session in those four weeks, it's a different story.

How to use the Running Rewired plan for YOUR needs

Tens of thousands of runners will use this plan, and it's my hope that they tailor it to their needs. Building a plan around *your* needs will require some big-picture planning to map the **macrocycle** that culminates with your next big goal. At the same time, I also want you to think about how this plan fits with your weekly run training, from one **microcycle** to the next, so that the work to be done aligns with three clear goals split into the following categories:

1. Build durable parts → PREHAB exercises
2. Build skilled movement for running → PRECISION workouts
3. Build strength and power → PERFORMANCE workouts

Drill work

Awareness matters. If you are looking for running cues + tips to ensure that the skills in this plan are successfully integrated into you running form, check out the Drills section following this chapter. Keep it simple. Instead of overloading your brain with 20 different ideas, pick one drill each run and see which tips resonate best with you. These drills reinforce the postural integrity and triple extension that are key to seeing running gains.

PREHAB WORKOUTS

The basis for these workouts is explained in Chapter 10. The movements are simple, but warrant a few key tips to ensure they are executed correctly:

Bone health

For optimal loading, do 40 jumps per leg before running. Yes, even *before* your warm-up run. You can choose to do the tendon-loading exercises or other precision exercises prior to these—just don't run. Choose a simple plyometric exercise to get the work done—I like the Split Box Jump (which can be done on a curb) or the Lateral Hurdle Hop (jumping over a

TABLE 11.1 The Running Rewired Program Overview

	Prehab	Precision	Performance
Benefit	Build robust bones and tendons	Move your body with control for durability	Increase force and rate of force generation
Frequency	2–3/week	1–2/week	1–2/week
Duration	10–12 min.	15–20 min.	45 min.
Stress	Low stress, may improve recovery	Low stress, may improve recovery	Higher load, will require recovery
Season Timing	All season	All season	Workouts 8–12 throughout the season, excluding the 4 weeks leading up to key races Workouts 14 + 15: Best incorporated in the 4 weeks prior to key races. All performance workouts can be skipped or done at 50% of volume in recovery weeks or leading up to lower-priority races. Workout 16 can be done anytime during the season.
Weekly Timing	Run/non-run days Use these exercises as a dynamic warm-up *Bone loading must be done pre-run*	Run/non-run days Workouts can be used as dynamic warm-up.	Anytime except for 2 days (48hrs) prior to your VO2 Run workout
Taper	Eliminate 2 weeks prior to key race	No change	Workouts 8–12: Omit in taper Workouts 14–16: Do 50% volume in 2-week lead-up to a key race

gym bag, clothes, or a log). It makes for a great dynamic warm-up. Remember, the key is to get off the ground *quickly*. You can break up the 40 jumps into sets of 8–10 jumps, taking 15 seconds of rest to ensure you jump explosively on every rep. Getting 40 jumps with rest as needed will take about 1.5–2 minutes.

Tendon health

These three exercises can be done pre-run, post run, or on a day when you aren't running. Remember the key to healthy tendons is *slow movement*. Spend 2–3 seconds on the way down, and an additional 2–3 seconds on the way back up for each rep. Slow, controlled movement takes priority over the load used, so use body weight to start.

If you are looking for progression, see the tips offered with each exercise description in Chapter 10. The use of the MOBO in the Helicopter Lunge and Calf Raise exercises improves your tissue loading, but these exercises can also be done without the board. You will need about 10 minutes to get these exercises done.

PRECISION WORKOUTS

These workouts (1–7) are designed to cue smooth movements and build better muscle memory. You can do these workouts in just 15–20 minutes with minimal equipment. In fact, Workouts 1 and 2 use just your body weight. If you have a Swiss ball, a TheraBand, a sling or other suspension system, a Powerband, and a MOBO, you can add those respective routines as a possible precision workout for the week. Because the body learns best with both repetition and some variety, don't do the same workout for each precision workout session, but make sure you repeat them from time to time.

The best time to do a precision workout is prior to a run—think of it as a dynamic warm-up. Using deliberate practice to cue muscles before a run is a great way to help you feel them on your run.

There is some evidence to show that precision workouts may actually accelerate recovery from your harder workouts during the week.

If you can't fit in a run or gym session but you want to do something, do one of the precision workouts twice through.

Workout 7, Hip Runs, includes running to help build a hip dominant pattern. You will do a circuit, then run, and repeat this pattern for a total of 3.25 miles. This is a good option for an easy day and particularly for runners who have a hard time integrating their hips into triple extension.

PERFORMANCE WORKOUTS

These workouts are designed around the principles of overload, specificity, and variability. They are grouped into three distinct purposes to elicit three distinct responses.

Workouts 8–11 build general strength and muscle recruitment. These staples could easily constitute an entire successful strength plan for the majority of runners. They become more challenging as you progress toward Workout 11. If you are new to lifting, rotate through these workouts for at least 9 months before attempting workouts 12–15. You will need a bigger baseline of strength to get the right stimulus from the other workouts. To increase the intensity of these workouts, use more weight.

Workouts 12–13 are compound workouts, which I only recommend for runners who have been doing gym work for over 9 months. Even though the volume of these workouts isn't higher, the combination of strength and plyometric movements demands a lot from your body. To increase intensity, try adding weight, but also increase the speed of your movement at the same time. This type of work pays off, but it is only effective at specific times of the season. These are best done in the period ramping up to high-intensity or high-volume training intensity, as well as in the pre-season and off-season.

Workouts 14–16 improve your power generation to the ground. Workouts 14 and 15 use body weight or mid-weight loads, but the emphasis is on fast, explosive movements. Workout 16 uses only the medball to help you specifically improve your horizontal force application. This one is actually pretty fun as well. Because the load is minimal, Workout 16 is a safe option even for newer runners to learn better movement speed. Best of all, it requires minimal equipment—just a medball.

Performance workouts will require about 45 minutes. This accounts for both the work and recovery time between sets, but it doesn't account for time spent talking or posting about your workout on social media! Admittedly, the exercises may take longer if you are not familiar with the movements. If this is the case, drop the number of sets for your first few workouts and pay strict attention to form. Unlike the precision workouts, these sessions will create fatigue and possibly impact your runs. Plan your key running workouts to be at least 48 hours out from performance training workout days. We don't want acute soreness from the gym to interfere with your most critical interval sessions of the week.

It's good practice to build recovery weeks into your training. While this varies from coach to coach, the typical approach involves three weeks at higher intensity and volume, followed by a lighter training load in week 4 to allow time for recovery. Your Running Rewired plan will follow the same schedule: Take a break from the performance workouts every fourth week, but continue the precision workouts. In the 4 weeks prior to key races, your performance workouts should be limited to the following:

- Workouts 8–11 and 16 for runners with less than 9 months of strength work
- Workouts #14,15,16 for runners with more than 9 months of strength work

Daily workout structure

All of the performance workouts are laid out in the same way:

CUE: Warm-up movements to prime your nervous system for work.

DRIVE: The main set is made up of key intensity and movement targets.

CORRECT: Add in 1–2 optional movements to correct imbalances or further develop skill and progress week over week (See Appendix, p. 285).

The Cue exercises improve your movement in anticipation of the quality work in the main set. You need an adequate warm-up, but not so much that you are fatigued before you get to the main set. The Drive exercises are where the work gets done to increase the skill of force production. They are generally 12-15 sets of total work. Technically, the workout is over at this point. However, this is where you can personalize your plan to better address your specific needs. In the Appendix you'll find all of the exercises categorized according to the skill they develop or the problem they solve. Each exercise is also categorized as Level 1 or Level 2 . For example, if you notice that you are struggling with rotational hip control, you can work on the Level 1 Glute Rainbow and Hip Circles exercises for a few weeks. And after those movements become easy, you might choose to progress to Level 2 hip rotation exercises. When you have the time, these corrective exercises are a great way to bend the plan to your specific needs.

Plan for Progression in Your Strength Workouts

The needle should always be moving, but it doesn't go up each day. No one knocks 5 seconds off their 400s every week, nor is it possible to add 10 pounds to your deadlift week over week. You will hit plateaus. But when you notice a plateau lasting longer than a few sessions, try breaking up the total work or set to get back to progress.

For the main set of each performance workout, I've indicated a rep count for each exercise that is generally around 8 reps. But feel free to make tweaks in the rep count to achieve the ultimate goal of improving your strength, or rate of force development. Here's an example:

Instead of squatting 3 x 8 reps at 155 pounds, try for 4 x 4 reps or 4 x 5 reps at 165 pounds. You are simply breaking up the total workload by doing less volume per set. This minor adjustment can minimize the fatigue and allow you to push harder or more explosively. For runners, I like to see sets of at least 4 reps, as we are never trying to push a max load. A few things happen when you manipulate your training this way—you will most likely improve your physiological strength capacity, but there can also be a mental advantage in knowing you can push harder and get past these plateaus. And when in doubt, always use a spotter!

The main sets of these workouts are supposed to be challenging. You don't go to the track and run at conversation pace during your key intervals of the week. Instead, you run hard, to the point that you *need* the rest between efforts. Please take note of the rest time indicated between sets in these plans. If you feel like you only need 30-45 seconds after each set, you aren't lifting with enough load or intensity. While there's no need to leave the gym in a stretcher since we aren't doing max effort work and you don't need to lift to failure every set, you should feel like you truly need that rest before doing the final rep of each set.

INTEGRATING YOUR PROGRAM WITH RUNNING

Successful training programs are designed to cycle, or periodize, the type of training over the season and throughout the week to hit all the key aspects of preparation. There are high volume and intensity blocks when we feel like walking zombies and lighter training to allow for recovery. But it all works to produce a super compensation in fitness and help you to peak for key races during the year. Because your strength and conditioning plan complements your physiological development, it is periodized, too.

The dosage of any activity is broken down into frequency, intensity, and duration. Each workout specifies intensity and durations to remove most of the guesswork. But you will need to know how to use these workouts throughout the year and each week.

Big-picture planning

Skills require practice, and just as our run training is ongoing, so is our rewiring. To refine your movement precision and build a bigger spring, you will need to perform this work 2–3 times per week, working around your run training. For recovery weeks, you only need to perform 1 precision workout.

In times of higher training load (later building phases and racing), this breaks down into 2 precision workouts and 1 performance workout per week, for a total of 1.5 hours per week.

In times of general fitness and volume building (generally the off-season and early building periods), perform 1 precision workout and 2 performance workouts, for a total of 2 hours per week.

When time is tight, do 1 precision and 1 performance workout per week, for a total of 70 minutes.

Running Intensity and Compatibility

In any given week, your run training typically falls into three different categories:

Aerobic intensity. These workouts deliver more blood flow to working muscles, and improve your body's efficiency at using energy to keep you running. A bigger aerobic engine enables you to run longer at a higher intensity before needing to tap the powerful but fatigue-inducing anaerobic fuel systems. Most of our training volume tends to fall into the aerobic category. The timing of your performance workouts is not affected by these aerobic workouts, at least to a point. Marathoners and ultra-runners can benefit from a buffer between their long runs. It's typically okay to do a performance workout before 48 hours of a long run, but avoid doing a performance workout 48 hours after a long run lasting more than 2.5 hours. So if your 2.5-hour long run is on Saturday, wait until Tuesday, not Monday, to do your performance workout.

Tempo work. Lactate gets a bad rap: Ultimately it's your friend, not your foe. It is an energy source that you can tap when the intensity needs to be turned up. However, when you use lactate for energy, it produces a bunch of acidic hydrogen ions that need to be cleared out of your body. Your muscles don't like to be filled up with acid. The goal of tempo work is to help you push the acid out of your cells so you can run faster, longer. Given that this type of run is done in the range of 7.5–10 on the intensity scale, and under 40 minutes, you shouldn't experience much interference from scheduling a performance workout within 48 hours of this run.

VO2max/high-intensity intervals. Some amazing things happen to your physiology when you push yourself to the max, both aerobically and anaerobically. But it doesn't take much volume to see improvements. Less than 20 minutes of your weekly training should be hard. This is a key workout of the week, and all volume, whether strength and conditioning or run training, should be adjusted to ensure that you arrive rested and ready to run at max (10 out of 10 on the intensity scale). Set your week up so that you do not do a performance workout 48 hours prior to a VO2max workout. The worst-case scenario would be to do your performance workout on Sunday and your VO2 max workout on Tuesday, as your performance in your key session may be compromised.

Timing between weekly workouts

Lifting and running are complementary, contrary to what's been preached in the past. However, it's critical that these workouts are timed appropriately to add up to better fitness. Peak soreness from strength and power work happens about 48 hours following your gym session, so it makes sense that you won't feel your best the day after, but your soreness will actually be greatest two days after.

In the best-case scenario, strength and plyometric training help activate the muscles. There are several studies to support the idea that lifting prior to running actually improves the quality of key running workouts executed on the same day. This is why I have my elite athletes lift in the morning, eat breakfast and rest for an hour or so, and then complete their running workouts. Typically these are the harder workouts of the week, including intervals and tempo work. If their schedule doesn't allow for this, then all other key run workouts are done at least 48 hours after the gym session. This prevents soreness from compromising hard runs later in the week.

Most working folks don't have the luxury of all this free time, but the same rules apply. Keep your hard runs 48 hours apart from hard gym sessions to make sure you can give it your all during these key runs, but it is okay to run low and moderate intensities on sore legs. If your schedule has you running in the day or two after going to the gym, make it an easy or tempo run because it places less strain on your muscles and promotes active recovery.

Lastly, soreness dissipates with time. If you are new to the gym, you may feel sore—quite sore!—after each of the performance workouts for the first 2–3 weeks. But fear not. After your body is exposed to the stressors of the gym for 3–4 weeks, your soreness from performance workouts should be a fraction of what you experience the first few sessions. If you have never stepped foot into the weight room, it's a good idea to take your time to master the form cues in this plan and gradually ramp up the weight use for each exercise. If you do have experience lifting, you likely remember how sore you were after your first day in the gym, and how your body adapted over time with less and less soreness after each gym session.

A Plan for New Runners

Running can seem simple—just put your shoes on and go! But as you've seen so far, there's a bit more to it if we want to keep your training consistent and keep pushing your performance.

Think back to the first day of high school, or a new job. You had an orientation where they threw so many rules, regulations, and novel information at you that your head was spinning! Even though it seemed like a lot at the time, you eventually fell into a routine.

This book is your orientation to the world of running. It's my goal to make sure you don't become an injury statistic. The reality is that 80 percent of runners get hurt, and almost half of all runners get hurt every year. I'd rather see you show up with a focused plan to wire your run correctly from the start. What follows is my advice on how to structure your running program.

Run in small bites

We all like snacks, but an all-you-can-eat buffet will leave you feeling all kinds of regret. It's similar with training. I know you have a friend who runs 18 miles every Saturday morning, but she's not you. It's much better to split your run volume into 2–4 days per week instead of binging on miles and training fewer days per week.

Strive for simplicity

You know what's great about being a beginner and having a beginner mindset? Your brain is like a sponge, and almost everything you do consistently will lead to success. This is why as a new runner, you don't need an elite coach. You need a simple plan to regularly get your butt out the door. As a beginner, aim to run 2–3 days each week. Make sure 2 of those days are at an easy conversational pace. This pace may start out as a run/walk workout as you build up endurance. Please know there's no shame in run/walk workouts. Everyone has to start somewhere, and those walk/run workouts build your fitness base.

Use intervals to unlock fitness

Running hard for a long time is *not* the best way to get good at running hard for a long time! When you run hard for a lot of miles, it takes a big toll on your body, which means you'll need a long time to recover. If your goal is to train consistently, this strategy puts that goal in jeopardy. Tempo intervals allow you to add a small volume of intensity to your training. Simply choose 1 of your 3 days of training to do a short warm-up of about 5–8 minutes of running. Then start your interval with a harder effort, called "on" time, followed by recovery. The goal of the interval is to hit a pace that feels like a 7/10 on the intensity scale. Start by holding that pace for about 1–3 minutes of on time, then recover with off time for as long as you need. The recovery can be an easy jog, a walk, or even sitting down. Your recovery needs to be as long as you need to be able to put in quality 7/10 efforts on the remaining intervals. And to start out, you should aim for a total of 12–15 minutes of "on" time. Obviously this can be done many different ways. You could do 12 x 1 minute intervals, or 4 x 3 minute intervals, or 6 x 2 minute tempo intervals. Just keep it simple and consistent. You don't need a track or a fancy watch; just get out there and put in the work. If you do your tempo interval workout right, you should not feel destroyed after it. The goal is a 7/10 pace.

The single biggest reason a training plan fails is because you mix up your plan with your friend's plan. Here's how this plays out in every city in the world. You are supposed to do an easy run—let's just that easy run was planned at a 9:45 pace/mile. That morning your friend, who's been running for a long time, says, "Hey I'm doing an easy run too—can I join you?" You are so excited and immediately agree to it! You meet up and start out for your "easy" run. You were planning on running 9:45 miles, but your friend is running 8:30 miles. You can keep up, but it's a struggle. That run was incredibly easy for your friend, but not you.

At one point you planned on doing intervals on Wednesday. If you had done an easy run on Monday, you would have shown up with a ton of energy and ready to crush those intervals. Instead, you show up tired from the previous workout. You can't push your intervals, so you run really slow. Not only did you show up to your key interval session exhausted, but since you couldn't put in quality work, you didn't earn quality fitness from your interval session. You can see how this cycle spins out of control, and instead of progressing, you wind up dragging yourself into and out of every run. Stop.

Keeping your easy days easy lets you put in quality efforts when the time is right. When your plan says do an easy run, make sure it's easy for you. When it's time for intervals, you need to show up ready to put in some effort. One note here, this isn't just newbie mistake—I've seen this happen in every ability level out there. Your training plan is YOUR plan.

Remember that volume is not "running currency"

Many runners believe their weekly mileage volume is just as important as their 401k. Stop it. I've alluded to this already, but I want to repeat it for your benefit: your weekly mileage is not the defining feature of you as a runner. Olympic medals have been won running as little as 35 miles a week. People love talking about volume, and that's a shame. Instead they should be talking about quality runs for their given fitness. As we mentioned, every run has a purpose. Show up for that purpose, over and over, and you'll see progress.

Everything is progressive, so enjoy the process

I've always told my athletes you are training today so you can train harder tomorrow. Everything is cumulative. Fitness builds on itself. After you've been running for a few years, you'll look at the times you just threw down on the track and think back to yourself, "There's no way I could have hit those splits one year ago!" And that's the whole idea. We want to continue pushing the needle, but doing it gradually.

1. Build skilled movement. As we said in Chapter 2, the goal is to go from cognitive to reflexive by building patterns from day 1. Day 1 is here. Focus on the precision workouts to build success.

2. Build better parts. As we've outlined in this book, running is going to place a lot of load, stress, and strain on your body. Simply running is not the best way to optimize your body parts for durability. The precision and performance exercises in this plan are not crosstraining in terms of general fitness. These plans are specifically developed to optimize your body for success in running.

3. **Monitor how you feel.** Taking note of how you feel is really important. I can't stand the phrase "listen to your body" because it has been circulating for decades, and I can tell you that most new runners don't know what to listen to! Instead let's make this simple with a 10-point scale. After each run, you should be able to score it. Easy runs should be in the 4–6 range on the scale. Your tempo intervals sessions should feel like a 7/10 effort (during the "on times"). If you were able to match that, then congrats, you nailed the point of that workout that day! But if you were supposed to run fast and the workout felt like a 3/10, you should have pushed harder. And if you ran your tempo intervals and gave it a 9/10 effort, you likely went a bit too hard. Note: The VO2 runs mentioned previously in this chapter should be run at a perceived exertion of 10/10 intensity, but you should give yourself at least 6–9 months before adding in these type of sessions. They are quite intense! And this self-monitoring tip still holds true if a VO2 session demands a 10/10 effort but you are exhausted with life stress in such a way that you feel like a 6/10 before you even put your shoes on; you may need to reevaluate your plan leading up to these workouts each week. You need to show up to those workouts ready to crush, not be crushed. Taking inventory of your effort is incredibly helpful for you to learn pacing and intensity.

I can't tell you how many times in my career that patients have told me, "I wish I knew this when I started running; it would have changed the way I train!" But that's not going to be you. Before long, you will be looking back at your performance and saying, "Wow—I did it."

Different plans for different runners

What follows are four different scenarios for four different types of runners to show how a week of training could be structured, along with specific tips for this type of runner. Note that each of these plans features a complete day of rest. To get the most of your training, work should be challenging. And we recover with rest!

TABLE 11.2 New + Fitness Runner Sample Weekly Schedule

New Runner (or Fitness Runner)	Run Rewired	Run Workout
Monday	Off	Off
Tuesday	Precision/Prehab	VO$_2$max workout
Wednesday	Performance workout	
Thursday	Prehab	Tempo
Friday	Performance workout (optional)	
Saturday	Precision	Long(ish) run
Sunday		Crosstrain

New Runner Notes: As mentioned previously in this chapter, newer runners should perform the PREHAB and PRECISION workouts as prescribed, but limit their PERFORMANCE workouts to 8–11 and 16 only. Crosstraining is included on the calendar one day per week. Other sports (especially ones that allow us to use multidirectional movements) yield so many benefits for bone density and movement skill. Notice the number of performance workouts. New runners definitely need one of these workouts each week, but there's an optional performance workout on Friday as well. A second performance session creates a more well-rounded training effect for general fitness.

TABLE 11.3 High School Runner Sample Weekly Schedule

High School Cross Country Runner (In-Season)	Run Rewired	Run Workout
Monday	Precision	VO$_2$max workout
Tuesday	Prehab	Easy run
Wednesday	Performance workout	Tempo
Thursday	Prehab	Hills
Friday	Precision	Short tempo with strides
Saturday		Race/time trial/workout
Sunday	Off	Off

High school runners present a real challenge, and it's hard to check all the boxes. The season is so short, and freshman and sophomores are still adjusting to their rapidly changing bodies. There's so much need for skill development and so little time. This group will benefit from two days of precision workouts. Adolescents need more movement skill exposure than other groups. I encourage coaches of high school runners to use these workouts as a dynamic warm-up for the run for those two days. From there, younger runners can maintain a slightly lower volume of strength and power work. If time is an issue, they can drop one set from each main set exercise (e.g., instead of 3 sets of dead lifts, perform just 2 sets). Young athletes require less volume to get improvements in force production.

TABLE 11.4 Masters Runner Sample Weekly Schedule

Masters Weekly	Run Rewired	Run Workout
Monday	Off	Off
Tuesday		VO$_2$max workout
Wednesday	Performance workout	1 mile easy
Thursday	Prehab	Tempo
Friday	Performance workout	
Saturday	Precision	Tempo
Sunday	Prehab	Long run

Note that masters runners have two performance workouts. If you recall the changes that we "typically" see in masters runners that were discussed in Chapter 10 you know why: Running isn't enough to maintain muscle mass, and there are corresponding changes in running form that come from this decreased force generation capacity. If there's a group of runners that most needs to embrace an emphasis on strength and power in training, it's masters runners. Let's keep your body moving well and feeling great.

TABLE 11.5 Elite Runner Sample Weekly Schedule

ELITE in Build Phase	Run Rewired	Run Workout
Monday	Prehab/Precision	Easy run
Tuesday	Performance workout (light)	VO$_2$max workout
Wednesday	Prehab	Easy with pick-ups
Thursday	Performance workout (intense)	Tempo
Friday	Precision	Long run
Saturday		Race/time trial/workout
Sunday	Off	Off

One tweak I often employ in programming for elite athletes is to separate strength workouts into light and intense sessions. Since the training load for these athletes is both quite high and quite intense at certain times of the season, we maintain the volume of strength work, but drop the intensity. We program a workout at 80 percent max intensity on the first day it's scheduled in the week, and then do the full intensity or volume in the second session.

For example, in this particular week the athlete will do the full Horizontal Focus workout at 80 percent of max intensity to rehearse form and muscle memory prior to their VO2max workout, then they repeat the same Horizontal Focus workout on Thursday at full intensity. This same scenario can be employed by anyone wishing to place a bit more emphasis on learning exercise form while keeping some volume, but slightly decreasing the intensity.

All four of these above scenarios maintain the same guidelines for the number of sessions and timing of those sessions, but make the organization and dosage more specific to the given group.

SOLIDIFYING THE BRAIN-BODY CONNECTION

I once heard a sports psychologist say, "You move the way you think—mental imagery and rehearsal actually improve the way you perform." Yes, mental imagery is an incredible and powerful tool that's been used for years to prep and refine muscle memory. But one step up from imagining better movement is to actually practice better movement.

Now that you are well into this program, your brain-body connection is being rewired for better running. When you trust your training and preparation, you don't have to force your best performance on race day . . . or worse, simply hope for it to happen. Each new skill you've practiced has made new connections and literally adapted your nervous system for reflexive movement. You know how to execute precision movement to steer your body under control. You can sustain the heavy loads that once threatened to crush your can, and you know how to maintain a powerful position for every stride of your run. Now it's time to use this brain-body connectivity to redefine your limits as a runner.

practice › plasticity › growth = rewired for success

Drill Work

Precision and performance workouts lay a foundation to improve the way you move. Adding in specific run drills and cues throughout the week helps solidify the skills that transfer to your running. These are quick, fun efforts that have a high bang-for-the-buck factor, and can be done before, after, or even during your run.

PRECISION STRIDE MECHANICS DRILLS

POSTURE CHECK

- Stop every mile or so and stand on one leg.

- Make sure that your weight is evenly split between heel and forefoot on both feet.

- If you are heavy on the heels, drop your ribs down slightly in front until you feel centered. Then drop your arms down to the sides and face the palms forward to help the shoulder blades slide down and back along your back.

- Maintain this posture as you take off again.

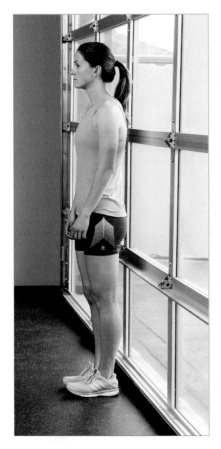 

PUSH VERSUS PULL

- Stand with your back to a wall (left photo), then step away from the wall. Feel your leg pushing into the wall to move forward (right photo).

- Practice this drill for a minute before you leave for your run to familiarize your body with the feeling of pushing (not pulling) your body forward—this simple concept will help you unlock your hips for a powerful stride.

FINGERTIP POSTURE DRILL

- Review the Posture Check (p. 210) to practice finding your neutral spine.

- Once you are in a neutral position, spread your fingers. Place your pinkies on the large bump in the front of your pelvis (your anterior superior iliac spine, or ASIS) and place your thumbs on any rib.

- Imagine your hands are vice grips locking your upper body position down over your pelvis and walk forward. Allow your thumbs and pinky fingers to cue your posture to remain stacked. Incorporate this drill throughout the day to build awareness, and even while running, using one hand to cue yourself into better alignment.

TIP

This may be the simplest cue to ensure your new core control transfers into your gait. The goal is to extend your hip behind you while keeping your torso stacked over your hips.

SHOPPING CART

- Imagine you are having a party for 50 of your closest friends. You are at the grocery and have 300 pounds of food loaded in your cart. To move it you can't just lift a foot and reach forward. You have to drive off the back leg.

- For better propulsion, visualize yourself pushing the cart down the road as you run.

ELBOW JAB

- Stand facing a wall or tree, only inches away.

- Now swing your arms. You will quickly learn that you cannot swing your arms forward much.

- Focus on swinging your arms farther backward. Imagine that you are trying to drive your elbows into the runner behind you. Jab your elbow back to initiate the swing, then relax and let gravity take the arm back down for you.

DON'T SWING OUT

We want to swing the arms in a way that counter-balances the trunk over the legs. Most runners who swing their arms excessively forward overstride to counter the arm movement. While we don't run with our arms, this drill trains you to run with more compact alignment to improve your trunk position.

▷ PLYO RUN PERFORMANCE DRILLS

FLIP FLOP & PUSH-UP SPRINTS

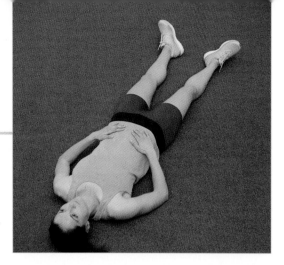

- This drill combines body coordination with acceleration.

- Start on your back. Once you are relaxed, flip yourself over into a lunge position and instantly accelerate into a full sprint for 20 meters.

- Take a 2-minute rest between each sprint, and aim for 6 repeats.

INCLINE SPRINTS

■ Running hills helps to cue proper form. For this drill, run 30-meter all-out sprints on a slight incline (2–4 percent grade), taking 2.5 minutes to rest in between each sprint. The rest is critical to ensuring that you hit peak velocity in each rep, so take the full rest. Aim to complete 4–6 reps.

STAIR BOUNDS

■ This drill can be done in a stadium or anywhere with several flights of steps. Using both legs on each jump and landing, explode up and forward, jumping up the stairs for 12 seconds. Do 5 sets with at least 90 seconds of rest in between each set. You can jump steps in succession or skip steps, but keep your time on the ground as short as possible. If you are double-bouncing while skipping steps, go back to doing quick jumps on every step.

OTHER PLYO RUN DRILLS

■ Ninja squat jumps and burpees (pp. 181, 185) can also be added within your run to help integrate muscle fiber recruitment. Use picnic benches, rocks, or downed trees as your box for the ninja jumps—do 2–4 sets of 6 reps. Or just find a patch of grass and sprinkle in sets of 6 burpees.

Prehab
Workouts

BONE LOADING

- 40 jumps, done pre-run, or non-run days.

OPTIONS
Split box jump or lateral hurdle hop

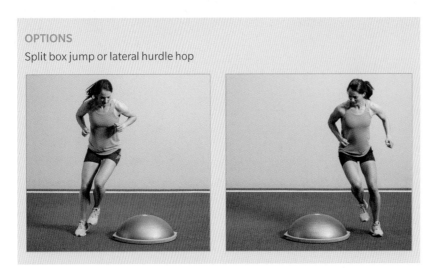

TENDON LOADING

- 24 total reps of each of these 3 exercises : Helicopter Lunge, Swiss Curl, and Calf Raise.

Precision
Workouts

Don't think of these workouts as a fitness routine and rush through them.
Practice skilled movement through your full range of motion.
Take 30–45 seconds rest between each exercise in the circuit.

3 rounds

Pigeon Hip Extension 10 reps on each side
Donkey Toes 20 reps on each leg, alternating
Tippy Twist 8 reps on each side

Frog Bridge 20 reps
Bear Walk 20 steps forward and backward
Lateral Hurdle Hop 20 hops
Burpees 10 reps

1

Pigeon Hip Extension   10 reps on each side   (p. 107)

2

Donkey Toes   20 reps on each leg, alternating   (p. 63)

3

Tippy Twist   8 reps on each side (p. 89)

4

Frog Bridge   20 reps (p. 108)

5

Bear Walk   20 steps forward and backward (p. 64)

6

Lateral Hurdle Hop 20 hops   (p. 183)

7

Burpees 10 reps   (p. 185)

2 rounds

Twisted Warrior 10 reps on each leg
Butt Scoots 20 reps on each side
Pigeon Hip Extension 10 reps on each side
Glute Rainbow 10 reps on each side

Standing Hip Circles 5 reps on each side
Tippy Twist 8 reps on each side
Burpees 10 reps
Frog Bridge 25 reps
Lateral Hurdle Hop 20 hops

1

Twisted Warrior 10 reps on each leg (p. 67)

2

Butt Scoots 20 reps on each side (p. 71)

3

Pigeon Hip Extension   10 reps on each side   (p. 107)

4

Glute Rainbow   10 reps on each side   (p. 76)

5

Standing Hip Circles   5 reps on each side   (p. 78)

6

Tippy Twist   8 reps on each side   (p. 89)

7

Burpees   10 reps   (p. 185)

8

Frog Bridge   25 reps   (p. 108)

Lateral Hurdle Hop   20 hops   (p. 183)

Banded Arm Circles 20 reps
Pull-Aparts 20 reps

CIRCUIT 2 rounds
Long Arm Band Squat 10 reps on each side
Banded Hip Twist 20 reps on each side
Bear Walk 30 steps forward and backward

Band Drive Thru 10 reps on each side
Thread the Needle Plank 20 reps on each side

Banded Arm Circles 20 reps
Pull-Aparts 20 reps

1

Banded Arm Circles 20 reps   (p. 51)

2

Pull-Aparts 20 reps   (p. 52)

3

Long Arm Band Squat   10 reps on each side   (p. 74)

4

Banded Hip Twist   20 reps on each side   (p. 77)

5

Bear Walk   30 steps forward and backward   (p. 64)

6

Band Drive Thru   10 reps on each side (p. 113)

7

Thread the Needle Plank   20 reps on each side (p. 73)

8

Banded Arm Circles   20 reps (p. 51)

9

Pull-Aparts   20 reps (p. 52)

TIME: 15–20 min.
EQUIPMENT: sling/suspension trainer

SLING CIRCUIT   4

SLING CIRCUIT

2 rounds

Sling Adductor 8 reps on each side
Sling Abductor 8 reps on each side
Rotisserie Chicken 8 reps on each leg
Reach Out 8 reps

Sling Push-Ups 8 reps
Sling Back Lunge 8 reps on each leg
Sling Row 8 reps
Sling Pistol Squat 8 reps on each leg

1

Sling Adductor   8 reps on each side   (p. 120)

2

Sling Abductor   8 reps on each side   (p. 119)

3

Rotisserie Chicken   8 reps on each side   (p. 81)

4

Reach Out   8 reps   (p. 62)

5

Sling Push-Ups   8 reps   (p. 174)

6

Sling Back Lunge   8 reps on each side   (p. 115)

7

Sling Row   8 reps   (p. 171)

8

Sling Pistol Squat   8 reps on each side   (p. 116)

BALL CIRCUIT

3 rounds

Twisted Warrior 10 reps on each leg
Ball Bridge Twist 20 reps
Donkey Toes 10 reps on each leg, alternating

Super Swiss Side Plank 10 reps on each side
Swiss Ball Tuck Twist 10 reps on each side
Tippy Twist 10 reps each leg
Push-Ups 10 reps

Twisted Warrior   10 reps on each leg   (p. 67)

Ball Bridge Twist   20 reps   (p. 69)

3

Donkey Toes   10 reps on each leg, alternating (Try it on a Swiss ball.)   (p. 63)

4

Super Swiss Side Plank   10 reps on each side   (p. 72)

5

Swiss Ball Tuck Twist   10 reps on each side   (p. 70)

6

Tippy Twist   10 reps on each leg   (p. 89)

7

Push-Ups   10 reps (Try putting your feet on a Swiss ball.)   (p. 173)

Foot Rocks 20 reps on each foot (both even and odd slots)

Foot Band Twist 30 reps

Star Squats 2 sets of 5 reps on each leg

Everted Pass Back 2 min. on each leg

Banded Foot Rocks 20 reps on each foot (both even and odd slots)

Foot Rocks   20 reps on each foot (both even and odd slots)   (p. 93)

Foot Band Twist   30 reps (both even and odd slots)   (p. 95)

3

Star Squats   2 sets of 5 reps on each leg (even slots)   (p. 97)

4

Everted Pass Back   2 min. on each leg (outer slots)   (p. 96)

5

Banded Foot Rocks   20 reps on each foot (even/odd slots)   (p. 94)

WARM-UP

Run 0.5 mile easy

HIP SERIES

Kneeling Banded Deadlift 10 reps
Band Drive Thru 8 reps on each side
Banded Hip Drag 8 reps on each side

Twisted Warrior 8 reps on each leg
Repeat Hip Series between each run.
- Run 0.25 mile easy
- Run 0.25 mile, building slowly to 80%
- Run 0.25 mile, building slowly to 90%
- Run 1 mile easy, with six 10-sec. surges to 80%
- Run 1 mile easy, with six 10-sec. surges to 80%

- Pay attention to form while shifting gears. This is more neuromuscular work than training.

WARM-UP

- Run 0.5 mile easy, then do Hip Series—this should take 2–3 minutes.

HIP SERIES

Kneeling Banded Deadlift 10 reps   (p. 112)

Band Drive Thru 8 reps on each side   (p. 113)

3

Banded Hip Drag   8 reps on each side   (p. 114)

4

Twisted Warrior   8 reps on each leg   (p. 67)

- Run 0.25 mile easy. Repeat Hip Series.
- Run 0.25 mile, building slowly to 80%. Repeat Hip Series.
- Run 0.25 mile, building slowly to 90%. Repeat Hip Series.
- Run 1 mile easy, with six 10-second surges to 80%. Repeat Hip Series.
- Run 1 mile easy, with six 10-second surges to 80%.

Performance
Strength
Workouts

Guidelines for performance workouts:

If you have never done strength training, cycle between Workouts 8–11 and Workout 16 for at least 3 months to build baseline skills.

If you have weight-lifting experience, select from Workouts 8–16. Note that Workouts 12 and 13 are quite taxing, and should not be deployed when training volume or intensity is at its peak.

In the 11–14 days preceding a peak race, continue the performance workouts, but at half volume. (The goal of a proper taper is to continue intensity while lowering volume. Research shows that RFD training is beneficial in tapering to produce super compensation.)

IN THIS SECTION

PERFORMANCE PREP

WARM-UP

Banded Arm Circles 20 reps
Pull-Aparts 20 reps
Overhead Carry 1 min.
Chair of Death Squat 25 reps
Single-Leg Deadlift with Dowel 25 reps on each side
Kettlebell Squat 20 reps

MAIN SET

Landmine Single-Leg Deadlift 3 × 8 reps on each side
Squat 3 × 8 reps
Kettlebell Swing 3 × 12 reps
Suitcase Carry 4 × 30-sec. carries, with 45 sec. rest

WARM-UP

■ Take a 30-second rest between each warm-up exercise.

1

Banded Arm Circles 20 reps (p. 51)

2

Pull-Aparts 20 reps (p. 52)

3

Overhead Carry 1 min.

(p. 50)

4

Chair of Death Squat 25 reps

(p. 109)

5

Single-Leg Deadlift with Dowel 25 reps on each side

(p. 111)

6

Kettlebell Squat   20 reps   (p. 167)

MAIN SET

■ For exercises 7-10, the goal is a 90- to 120-second rest between exercises unless otherwise stated.

7

Landmine Single-Leg Deadlift   3 x 8 reps (each side)   (p. 162)

8

Squat   3 × 8 reps (Set up a bench behind you to cue depth.)   (p. 169)

9

Kettlebell Swing   3 × 12 reps   (p. 166)

10

Suitcase Carry   4 × 30-sec carries (2 on each side) with 45 sec. rest   (p. 176)

SINGLE-LEG FOCUS

WARM-UP

Medball Twist 80 reps
Super Swiss Side Plank 25 reps on each side
Long Arm Band Squat 20 reps on each side
Archer Press Bridge 2 × 8 reps on each side

MAIN SET

Landmine Single-Leg Deadlift 3 × 8 reps on each side
Split Squat 3 × 8 reps on each side
Hip Thrust 3 × 8 reps
Waiter Carry 2 × 30-sec. reps on each side

WARM-UP

■ Take a 30-second rest between each warm-up exercise.

1

Medball Twist 80 reps
(p. 68)

2

Super Swiss Side Plank 25 reps on each side
(p. 72)

3

Long Arm Band Squat   20 reps on each side   (p. 74)

4

Archer Press Bridge   2 × 8 reps on each side   (p. 172)

MAIN SET

■ For exercises 5–8, the goal is a 90- to 120-second rest between exercises unless otherwise stated.

5

Landmine Single-Leg Deadlift   3 × 8 reps on each side   (p. 162)

6

Split Squat   3 × 8 reps on each side   (p. 168)

7

Hip Thrust 3 × 8 reps (p. 165)

8

Waiter Carry 2 × 30-sec. reps on each side (p. 175)

HORIZONTAL FORCE

WARM-UP

Long Arm Band Squat 20 reps on each side
Thread the Needle Plank 20 reps on each side
Archer Press Bridge 2 × 8 reps on each side
Split Box Jump 10 reps on each leg, alternating

MAIN SET

Romanian Deadlift 3 × 8 reps
Kettlebell Swing 3 × 8 reps
Hip Thrust 3 × 8 reps
Farmer Carry 3 × 40-sec. walks

WARM-UP

- Take a 30-second rest between each warm-up exercise.

1

Long Arm Band Squat   20 reps on each side   (p. 74)

2

Thread the Needle Plank   20 reps on each side   (p. 73)

3

Archer Press Bridge   2 × 8 reps on each side   (p. 172)

4

Split Box Jump   10 reps on each leg, alternating   (p. 184)

MAIN SET

■ For exercises 5–8, the goal is a 90- to 120-second rest between exercises unless otherwise stated.

5

Romanian Deadlift   3 × 8 reps   (p. 163)

6

Kettlebell Swing   3 × 8 reps   (p. 166)

7

Hip Thrust   3 × 8 reps   (p. 165)

8

Farmer Carry   3 × 40-sec. walks   (p. 177)

VERTICAL FORCE

WARM-UP

Rotisserie Chicken 8 reps on each side
Reach Out 20 reps
Hang Spine Twist 40 reps
Kettlebell Squat 3 × 8 reps

MAIN SET

Squat 4 × 8 reps
Banded Tippy Bird 3 × 10 each leg
Box Squat Jump 4 × 8 reps
Farmer Carry 3 × 40-sec. walks

WARM-UP

■ Take a 30-second rest between each warm-up exercise.

1

Rotisserie Chicken   8 reps on each side   (p. 81)

2

Reach Out   20 reps   (p. 62)

3

Hang Spine Twist   40 reps   (p. 75)

4

Kettlebell Squat   3 x 8 reps   (p. 167)

VERTICAL FORCE

MAIN SET

■ For exercises 5–8, the goal is a 90- to 120-second rest between exercises unless otherwise stated.

5

Squat   4 × 8 reps   (p. 169)

6

Banded Tippy Bird   3 × 10 each leg   (p. 80)

7

Box Squat Jump   4 × 8 reps   (p. 182)

8

Farmer Carry   3 × 40-sec. walks   (p. 177)

COMPOUND A

WARM-UP

Twisted Warrior 10 reps on each leg
Super Swiss Side Plank 25 reps
Reach Out 20 reps

COMPLEX SET 1 4 rounds

Kettlebell Squat 6 reps, rest 30 sec
Romanian Deadlift 8 reps, rest 30 sec
Lateral Hurdle Hop 20 hops, then rest 2 min

COMPLEX SET 2 3 rounds

Landmine Single-Leg Deadlift 8 reps on each side, rest 30 sec
Kettlebell Swing 10 reps, rest 30 sec
Split Box Jump 5 reps on each side, then rest 2 min.

1

Twisted Warrior 10 reps on each leg   (p. 67)

2

Super Swiss Side Plank 25 reps on each side   (p. 72)

3

Reach Out   20 reps   (p. 62)

COMPLEX SET 1   4 rounds of exercises 4–6

■ For exercises 4–9, the goal is a 30-second rest between exercises, and a 2-minute break between rounds

4

Kettlebell Squat   6 reps   (p. 167)

COMPOUND A

5

Romanian Deadlift   8 reps   (p. 163)

6

Lateral Hurdle Hop   20 hops, then rest 2 mins.   (p. 183)

COMPLEX SET 2 3 rounds of exercises 7–9

7

Landmine Single-Leg Deadlift   8 reps on each side   (p. 162)

8

Kettlebell Swing   10 reps   (p. 166)

Split Box Jump   5 reps on each side, then rest 2 mins.   (p. 184)

WARM-UP

Swiss Ball Tuck Twist 3 × 30 sec.
Sling Push-Ups 2 × 12 reps
Banded Hip Jacks 3 × 30 sec. on each side, with 10 jacks in between

COMPLEX SET 1 4 rounds

Romanian Deadlift 6 reps, rest 30 sec.
Box Squat Jump 6 reps, rest 2 min.

COMPLEX SET 2 3 rounds

Split Squat 6 reps on each side, rest 30 sec.
Ninja Squat Jump 6 reps, rest 1 min.

Banded Tippy Bird 3 × 8 reps on each leg
Archer Press Bridge 2 × 8 reps on each side

WARM-UP

■ Take a 30-second rest between each warm-up exercise.

1

Swiss Ball Tuck Twist   3 × 30 sec.   (p. 70)

2

Sling Push-Ups   2 × 12 reps   (p. 174)

3

Banded Hip Jacks   3 × 30 sec. on each side, with 10 jacks in between   (p. 117)

■ For exercises 4–5, the goal is a 45-second rest between exercises, and a 2-min. break between rounds

COMPLEX SET 1 4 rounds of exercises 4–5

4

Romanian Deadlift   6 reps, rest 30 sec.   (p. 163)

5

Box Squat Jump   6 reps, rest 2 mins.   (p. 182)

COMPLEX 2   3 rounds of exercises 6–7

6

Split Squat   6 reps on each side, rest 30 sec.   (p. 168)

7

Ninja Squat Jump   6 reps, rest 1 min.   (p. 181)

8

Banded Tippy Bird   3 × 8 each leg

(p. 80)

9

Archer Press Bridge   2 × 8 reps on each side

(p. 172)

Performance
Power
Workouts

Power workouts are best used in the rotation approximately 6 weeks from the peak race of the season.

WARM-UP
Long Arm Band Squat 20 reps on each side
Hang Spine Twist 25 reps on each side
Swiss Ball Tuck Twist 3 × 30 sec.
Split Squat 3 × 8 on each leg

JUMP BLOCK
Box Squat Jump 3 × 5 reps
Split Box Jump 5 reps on each side

POWER SPEED SET
Do these 3 lifts at 40% of weight max.
Romanian Deadlift 3 × 5 reps
Dumbbell Push Press 3 × 4 reps on each leg
Hip Thrust 3 × 6 reps

1

Long Arm Band Squat   20 reps on each side   (p. 74)

2

Hang Spine Twist   25 reps on each side   (p. 75)

3

Swiss Ball Tuck Twist   3 × 30 sec.   (p. 70)

4

Split Squat   3 × 8 reps on each leg   (p. 168)

JUMP BLOCK

5

Box Squat Jump   3 × 5 reps   (p. 182)

6

Split Box Jump   5 reps on each side   (p. 184)

POWER SPEED SET

■ Do these 3 lifts at 40% of weight max. Rest as needed to explode

7

Romanian Deadlift   3 × 5 reps: 2 count down, explode on drive up   (p. 163)

8

Dumbbell Push Press   3 × 4 reps on each leg: sink and explode up   (p. 180)

POWER A

9

Hip Thrust   3 × 6 reps: explode up   (p. 165)

WARM-UP

Butt Scoots 3 × 10 reps
Kneeling Banded Deadlift 30 reps
Dumbbell Push Press 3 × 5 reps on each leg

COMPLEX SET 5 rounds

Squat 5 reps at 40% weight, rest 30 sec.
Box Squat Jump 3 reps, rest 90 sec.

Kettlebell Swing 3 × 8 reps
Burpee 3 × 6 reps
Sling Back Lunge 2 × 10 reps on each leg

1

Butt Scoots 3 × 10 reps   (p. 71)

2

Kneeling Banded Deadlift 30 reps   (p. 112)

3

Dumbbell Push Press   3 × 5 reps on each leg   (p. 180)

COMPLEX SET   5 rounds of exercises 4–5

4

Squat   5 reps at 40% weight, rest 30 sec.; 2-count on the way down, then explode up   (p. 169)

5

Box Squat Jump 3 reps, rest 90 sec.   (p. 182)

6

Kettlebell Swing 3 × 8 reps   (p. 166)

7

Burpees 3 × 6 reps   (p. 185)

Sling Back Lunge   2 × 10 reps on each leg

(p. 115)

WARM-UP

- Run 5 min. easy

Medball Twist 40 reps

MAIN SET

- Do 3 sets of each exercise, then rest 1 min. before beginning the next exercise.

Medball Twist 'N' Cut 3 × 8 throws
Medball Triple Bound 3 × 2 reps
Medball Acceleration Sprint 3 × 2 reps
Medball Push Press 3 × 5 throws
Medball Granny Toss 3 × 5 throws

WARM-UP

- Run 5 minutes easy.

1

Medball Twist   40 reps   (p. 68)

MAIN SET

- Do 3 sets of each exercise, then rest 1 minute before beginning the next exercise.

2

Medball Twist 'N' Cut   3 × 8 throws   (p. 189)

3

Medball Triple Bound   3 × 2 reps   (p.190)

4

Medball Acceleration Sprint   3 × 2 reps   (p.191)

5

Medball Push Press   3 × 5 throws   (p. 187)

6

Medball Granny Toss   3 × 5 throws   (p. 188)

Appendix

Here you can find corrective exercises to customize your Running Rewired program. Simply choose a couple of exercises, starting with Level 1, then increase reps and/or load until you are ready for Level 2.

Acknowledgments

My dad once told me, "Your interest in writing is worth pursuing." At the time I had no idea where it would take me, how I would find opportunities, what I would write about, or whether it would be any good. But his advice has always stayed in my head. Thanks for the inspiration, Dad.

I'd like to thank Dr. Ron Smith, Dr. Robert Rowe, and the late Dr. David Pariser, all of whom expanded my brain in school. You not only made a mark on me as a student, but you helped shape my vision for the kind of teacher and clinician I strive to be. I'd also like to thank my undergraduate anatomy teacher. I hated your anatomy class and it made me doubt my career choice, but that experience gave me a desire to prove that learning doesn't have to be a one-dimensional experience of scribbling notes at 200 words per minute. When I taught undergraduate anatomy and other courses years later, my mission was to make clinical science engaging, innovative, applicable, and fun. To my professors, thanks for the passion.

I owe my entire practice and career to a decision by Dr. Casey Kerrigan, Dr. Bob Wilder, and James Myers to launch my vision of the most radical concept in sports medicine. Together, we launched the University of Virginia SPEED Clinic to use biomechanical analysis to solve the problems of endurance athletes. Our think tank of Dr. Ugo Della Croce, Eric Magrum, Dr. Jay Hertel, Dr. Chris Ingersol, Gabriele Paolini, Dr. Jason Franz, Dr. Corey Rynders, the late Jim Beazell, and a host of collaborators from research departments in the United States and abroad forever changed my thought process. We challenged each other by asking the right questions to help us discover better interventions for athletes, and it's my goal to share these lessons learned to pay it forward. Thanks to my current community at Oregon State University-Cascades and Boss Sports Performance for continuing this dream and creating an integrated solution for helping each athlete reach his or her potential. To my students, thanks for challenging us, your faculty, to send you out into the world ready to make a difference. Teaching the future is the most gratifying job I've ever had, and you make me proud. To all my patients and athletes over the decades, thanks for putting in the work to get where you wanted to go. Finally, thanks to my family for putting up with my crazy schedule, making me laugh, and joining me on my adventures in this wacky game called life. I'm continually your biggest fan. Collectively, these experiences have shaped my approach to rehab and performance training, and it is the basis for Running Rewired.

Which brings us to the writing of this book. My sincerest thanks to Renee Jardine, Kara Mannix, Vicki Hopewell, Andy Read, and the entire VeloPress team for your vision. You are all amazing at what you do. Renee, I don't know of many professionals out there who are as competent at their craft as you are at yours. If there's an Olympic medal for the most outstanding editor, you'll stand atop the podium every four years. Thanks to Jeff Clark, Livingston MacLake, and Lane Pearson for bringing these photos to life. And thanks to models Jen Luebke, Mel Lawrence, and Michael Olsen for bringing these movements and exercises to life. At the start, my editor, Renee, said that the sum of this book would be great. It is. Thanks.

To all the patients, athletes, coaches, clinicians, and sports scientists: Keep asking questions. Together, we will remain focused on the mission to find answers.

References

Alentorn-Geli, E. "The Association of Recreational and Competitive Running with Hip and Knee Osteoarthritis: A Systematic Review and Meta-Analysis." *Journal of Orthopaedic & Sports Physical Therapy* 47, 6 (June 2017)):373–390.

Brüggemann, et. al. "Effect of Increased Mechanical Stimuli on Foot Muscles Functional Capacity," ISB XXth Congress - ASB 29th Annual Meeting, 2005.

Chinn, L., J. Dicharry, J. Hart, J., S. Saliba, R. Wilder, and J. Hertel. "Gait Kinematics After Taping in Subjects with Chronic Ankle Instability." *Journal of Athletic Training* 49, 3 (May 2014): 322–330.

Chinn, L., J. Dicharry, and J. Hertel. "Ankle Kinematics of Individuals with Chronic Ankle Instability While Walking and Jogging on a Treadmill with Shoes." *Physical Therapy in Sport* 14, 4 (2013): 232–239.

Cook, J. "Revisiting the Continuum Model of Tendon Pathology: What Is Its Merit in Clinical Practice and Research?" *British Journal of Sports Medicine* 50 (2016): 1187–1191.

Dicharry, J. *Anatomy for Runners: Unlocking Your Athletic Potential for Health, Speed, and Injury Prevention.* New York: Sky Horse Publishing, 2012.

Dicharry, J. "Clinical Gait Analysis." In Robert Wilder, Francis O'Connor, and Eric Magrum, *Running Medicine,* 2nd ed. Monterey, CA: Healthy Learning, 2014.

Dicharry, J. "Kinematics and Kinetics of Gait: From Lab to Clinic." *Clinical Sports Medicine* 29, 3 (July 2010): 347–364.

Dugan, S. A., and K. P. Bhat. "Biomechanics and Analysis of Running Gait." *Physical Medicine and Rehabilitation Clinics of North America* 16, 3 (August 2005): 603–621.

Fletcher, J. R., S. P. Esau, and B. R. MacIntosh. "Changes in Tendon Stiffness and Running Economy in Highly Trained Distance Runners." *European Journal of Applied Physiology* 110, 5 (November 2010): 1037–1046.

Fredericson, M., + A. Nattiv. "The Healthy Runner Study." 2018 PAC-12 Student Athlete and Well-being Grant Program Presentation.

Goldmann J. P., Sanno, M., Willwacher, S, Heinrich, K., and Bruggerman, G. "The Potential of Toe Flexor Muscles to Enhance Performance." *Journal of Sports Sciences* 31, 4 (2013): 424–433.

Headlee, et. al. "Fatigue of the Plantar Intrinsic Foot Muscles Increases Navicular Drop." *Journal of Electromyography and Kinesiology* 18, 3 (2008): 420–425.

Herb, C. C., L. Chinn, J. Dicharry, P. O. McKeon, J. Hart, and J. Hertel. "Shank-Rearfoot Joint Coupling with Chronic Ankle Instability." *Journal of Applied Biomechanics* 30, 3 (June 2014): 366–372.

Hreljac, A. "Impact and Overuse Injuries in Runners." *Medicine and Science in Sports and Exercise* 36, 5 (May 2004): 845–849.

Hreljac, A., R. N. Marshall, and P. A. Hume. "Evaluation of Lower Extremity Overuse Injury Potential in Runners." *Medicine and Science in Sports and Exercise* 32, 9 (September 2000): 1635–1641.

Kelly, L. A. et al. "Recruitment of the Plantar Intrinsic Foot Muscles with Increasing Postural Demand." *Clinical Biomechanics* 27, 1 (2012): 46–51.

Kelly, A. et al. "Intrinsic Foot Muscles Have the Capacity to Control Deformation of the Longitudinal Arch." *Journal of the Royal Society Interface* 11 (2014): p. 93.

Kerdok, A. E., A. A. Biewener, T. A., McMahon, P. G. Weyand, and H. M. Herr. "Energetics and Mechanics of Human Running on Surfaces of Different Stiffnesses." *Journal of Applied Physiology* 92, 2 (February 2002): 469–478.

Kerrigan, D. C., and U. Della Croce. "Gait Analysis." Pp. 126–130 in F. G. O'Conner, Robert Sallis, Robert Wilder, and Patrick St. Pierre, eds., *Sports Medicine: Just the Facts.* New York: McGraw Hill, 2004.

Khan, K, Scott, A. "Mechanotherapy: How Physical Therapists' Prescription of Exercise Promotes Tissue Repair." *British Journal of Sports Medicine* 43, 4 (April 2009): 247–252.

Kongsgaard, M, et al. "Region Specific Patellar Tendon Hypertrophy in Humans Following Resistance Training." *Acta Physiologica* 191.2 (2007): 111–121.

Kram, R. "Bouncing to Conclusions: Clear Evidence for the Metabolic Cost of Generating Muscular Force." *Journal of Applied Physiology* 110, 4 (April 2011): 865–866.

Kram, R., and C. R. Taylor. "Energetics of Running: A New Perspective." *Nature* 346 (July 19, 1990): 265–267.

Laurersen, J. "The Effectiveness of Exercise Interventions to Prevent Sports Injuries: A Systematic Review and Meta-Analysis of Randomized Controlled Trials." *British Journal of Sports Medicine* 48, 11 (June 2014): 871–877.

McMahon, G. "No Strain, No Gain? The Role of Strain and Load Magnitude in Human Tendon Responses and Adaptation to Loading." *The Journal of Strength & Conditioning Research* 36, 10 (October 2022): 2950–2956.

Mountjoy, M., et al. "2023 International Olympic Committee Consensus statement on Relative Energy Deficiency in Sport (REDs)." *British Journal of Sports Medicine* 57 (2023): 1073–1097. doi:10.1136/bjsports-2023-106994.

Mousavi, S. "Kinematic Risk Factors for Lower Limb Tendinopathy in Distance Runners: A Systematic Review and Meta-Analysis." *Gait Posture* 69 (March 2019): 13–24.

Munteanu, S., and C. J. Barton. "Lower Limb Biomechanics during Running in Individuals with Achilles Tendinopathy: A Systematic Review." *Journal of Foot and Ankle Research* 4, 15 (2011).

Martin, P. E., and D. W. Morgan. "Biomechanical Considerations for Economical Walking and Running." *Medicine and Science in Sports and Exercise* 24, 4 (1992): 467–474.

Novacheck, T. F. "The Biomechanics of Running." *Gait and Posture* 7 (1998): 77–95.

Riley, P. O., J. Dicharry, J. Franz, U. D. Croce, R. P. Wilder, and D. C. Kerrigan. "A Kinematics and Kinetic Comparison of Overground and Treadmill Running." *Medicine and Science in Sports and Exercise* 40, 6 (June 2008): 1093–1100.

Riley, P. O., J. Franz, J. Dicharry, and D. C. Kerrigan. "Changes in Hip Joint Muscle-Tendon Lengths with Mode of Locomotion." *Gait and Posture* 31, 2 (February 2010): 279–283.

Roberts, T. J., R. L. Marsh, P. G. Weyand, and C. R. Taylor. "Muscular Force in Running Turkeys: The Economy of Minimizing Work." *Science* 275 (February 1997): 1113–1115.

Saunders, P. U., D. B. Pyne, R. D. Telford, and J. A. Hawley. "Factors Affecting Running Economy in Trained Distance Runners." *Sports Medicine* 34, 7 (2004): 465–485.

Saunders, P., et al. "Reliability and Variability of Running Economy in Elite Distance Runners." *Medicine and Science in Sports and Exercise* 36, 11 (November 2004): 1972–1976.

Suda, E., Watari, R., Matias, A., Taddei, U., and Sacco, I. "Predictive Effect of Well-Known Risk Factors + Foot Core Training in Lower Limb Running-Related Injuries in Recreational Runners: A Secondary Analysis of a Randomized Controlled Trial." *American Journal of Sports Medicine* 50, 1 (2022): 248–254.

Suloska, et al. "The Influence of Plantar Short Foot Muscle Exercises on the Lower Extremity Muscle Strength and Power in Proximal Segments of the Kinematic Chain in Long-Distance Runners." BioMed Research International (2019).

Taddei, U., Matian, A., Duarte, M., and Sacco, I. "Foot Core Training to Prevent Running Related Injuries: A Survival Analysis of a Single-Blind, Randomized Controlled Trial." *American Journal of Sports Medicine* 48, 14 (2020): 3610–3619.

Telhan, G., J. R. Franz, J. Dicharry, R. P. Wilder, P. O. Riley, and D. C. Kerrigan. "Lower Limb Joint Kinetics During Moderately Sloped Running." *Journal of Athletic Training* 45, 1 (January/February 2010): 16–21.

Tenforde, A., et al. "Participation in Ball Sports May Represent a Prehabilitation Strategy to Prevent Future Stress Fractures and Promote Bone Health in Young Athletes." *PMR* 7, 2 (February 2015): 222–225.

Watt, J. R., J. Franz, K. Jackson, J. Dicharry, and D. C. Kerrigan. "A Three-Dimensional Kinematic and Kinetic Comparison of Over Ground and Treadmill Walking in Healthy Elderly Subjects." *Clinical Biomechanics* 25, 5 (June 2010): 444–449.

Zelik, K. E., and A. D. Kuo. "Human Walking Isn't All Hard Work: Evidence of Soft Tissue Contributions to Energy Dissipation and Return." *Journal of Experimental Biology* 213 (December 2010): 4257–4264.

RUNNING SKILLS

Biewener, A. A., C. T. Farley, T. J. Roberts, and M. Temaner. "Muscle Mechanical Advantage of Human Walking and Running: Implications for Energy Cost." *Journal of Applied Physiology* 97, 6 (2004): 2266–2274.

Birrer, R.B., S. Buzermanis, M. P. DelaCorte, et al. "Biomechanics of Running." Pp. 11–19 in F. O'Connor and R. Wilder, eds., *The Textbook of Running Medicine.* New York: McGraw Hill, 2001.

Brown, A. M., R. A. Zifchock, and H. J. Hillstrom. "The Effects of Limb Dominance and Fatigue on Running Biomechanics." *Gait and Posture* 39, 3 (March 2014): 915–919.

Crowell, H. P., and I. S. Davis. "Gait Retraining to Reduce Lower Extremity Loading in Runners." *Clinical Biomechanics* 26, 1 (January 2011): 78–83.

Crowell, H. P., C. E. Milner, J. Hamill, and I. S. Davis. "Reducing Impact Loading During Running with the Use of Real-Time Visual Feedback." *Journal of Orthopaedic and Sports Physical Therapy* 40, 4 (April 2010): 206–213.

Davis, I. 2005. "Gait Retraining in Runners." *Orthopaedic Practice* 17, 2: 8–13.

Dean, J. C., and A. D. Kuo. "Energetic Costs of Producing Muscle Work and Force in a Cyclical Human Bouncing Task." *Journal of Applied Physiology* 110, 4 (April 2011): 873–880.

Dicharry, J. *Anatomy for Runners: Unlocking Your Athletic Potential for Health, Speed, and Injury Prevention.* New York: Sky Horse Publishing, 2012.

Dicharry, J. "Clinical Gait Analysis." In Robert Wilder, Francis O'Connor, and Eric Magrum, *Running Medicine*, 2nd ed. Monterey, CA: Healthy Learning, 2014.

Dicharry, J. "Kinematics and Kinetics of Gait: From Lab to Clinic." *Clinical Sports Medicine* 29, 3 (July 2010): 347–364.

Dicharry, J., J. R. Franz, R. P. Wilder, P. O. Riley, and D. C. Kerrigan. "Differences in Static and Dynamic Measures in Evaluation of Talonavicular Mobility in Gait." *Journal of Orthopaedic and Sports Physical Therapy* 39, 8 (2009): 628–634.

Franz, J. R., K. W. Paylo, J. Dicharry, P. O. Riley, and D. C. Kerrigan. "Changes in the Coordination of Hip and Pelvis Kinematics with Mode of Locomotion." *Gait and Posture* 29, 3 (2009): 494–498.

Hart, J. M., D. C. Kerrigan, J. M. Fritz, E. N. Saliba, B. Gansneder, and C. D. Ingersoll. "Jogging Gait Kinetics Following Fatiguing Lumbar Paraspinal Exercise." *Journal of Electromyography and Kinesiology* 19, 6 (December 2009): 458–464.

Honert, E., F. Ostermair, V. von Tscharner, and B. Nigg. "Changes in Ankle Work, Foot Work, and Tibialis Anterior Activation throughout a Long Run." *Journal of Sport and Health Science* 11, 3 (May 2022): 330–338.

Ireland, M. L. "The Female ACL: Why Is It More Prone to Injury?" *Orthopedic Clinics of North America* 33, 4 (October 2002): 637–651.

Ireland, M. L., and S. M. Ott. "Special Concerns of the Female Athlete." *Clinical Sports Medicine* 23, 2 (April 2004): 281–298.Leetun, D. T., M. L. Ireland, J. D. Willson, B. T. Ballantyne, and I. M. Davis. "Core Stability Measures as Risk Factors for Lower Extremity Injury in Athletes." *Medicine and Science in Sports and Exercise* 36, 6 (June 2004): 926–934.

McCann, D. J., and B. K. Higginson. "Training to Maximize Economy of Motion in Running Gait." *Current Sports Medicine Reports* 7, 3 (May 2008): 158–162.Milner, C. E., R. Ferber, C. D. Pollard, J. Hamill, and I. S. Davis. "Biomechanical Factors Associated with Tibial Stress Fracture in Female Runners." *Medicine and Science in Sports and Exercise* 38, 2 (February 2006): 323–328.

Milner, C. E., J. Hamill, and I. Davis. "Are Knee Mechanics During Early Stance Related to Tibial Stress Fracture in Runners?" *Clinical Biomechanics* 22, 6 (July 2007): 697–703.

Nigg, B. M. "The Role of Impact Forces and Foot Pronation: A New Paradigm." *Clinical Journal of Sports Medicine* 11, 1 (January 2001): 2–9.

Noehren, B., J. Scholz, and I. Davis. "The Effect of Real-Time Gait Retraining on Hip Kinematics, Pain and Function in Subjects with Patellofemoral Pain Syndrome." *British Journal of Sports Medicine* 45, 9 (July 2011): 691–696.

Rendos, N. K., B. C. Harrison, J. Dicharry, L. D. Sauer, and J. M. Hart. "Sagittal Plane Kinematics During the Transition Run in Triathletes." *Journal of Science and Medicine in Sport* 16, 3 (May 2013): 259–265.

Souza, R. B., and C. M. Powers. "Differences in Hip Kinematics, Muscle Strength, and Muscle Activation Between Subjects with and without Patellofemoral Pain." *Journal of Orthopaedic and Sports Physical Therapy* 39, 1 (January 2009): 12–19.

Suoza R. "Predictors of Hip Internal Rotation During Running: An Evaluation of Hip Strength and Femoral Structure in Women with and without Patellofemoral Pain." *American Journal of Sports Medicine* 37, 3 (March 2009): 579–587.

Teng, H. L., and C. M. Powers. "Influence of Trunk Posture on Lower Extremity Energetics During Running." *Medicine and Science in Sports and Exercise* 47, 3 (March 2015): 625–630.

Teng, H. "Sagittal Plane Trunk Posture Influences Patellofemoral Joint Stress During Running." *Journal of Orthopaedic and Sports Physical Therapy* 44, 10 (October 2014): 785–792.

Teunissen, L., A. Grabowski, and R. Kram. "The Effects of Independently Altering Body Weight and Body Mass on the Metabolic Cost of Running." *Journal of Experimental Biology* 210 (2007): 4418–4427.

Watt, J. R., K. Jackson, J. R. Franz, J. Dicharry, J. Evans, and D. C. Kerrigan. "Effect of a Supervised Hip Flexor Stretching Program on Gait in Frail Elderly Patients." *PM & R: The Journal of Injury, Function, and Rehabilitation* 3, 4 (April 2011): 330–335.

Wright, S., and P. G. Weyand. "The Application of Ground Force Explains the Energetic Cost of Running Backward and Forward." *Journal of Experimental Biology* 204 (2001): 1805–1815.

Zifchock, R. A., I. Davis, and J. Hamill. "Kinetic Asymmetry in Female Runners with and without Retrospective Tibial Stress Fractures." *Journal of Biomechanics* 39, 15 (2006): 2792–2797.

STRENGTH

Berryman, N., D. B. Maurel, and R. Bosquet. "Effect of Plyometric vs. Dynamic Weight Training on the Energy Cost of Running." *Journal of Strength and Conditioning Research* 24 (2010): 1818–1825.

Creer, A. R., M. D. Ricard, R. K. Conlee, G. L. Hoyt, and A. C. Parcell. "Neural, Metabolic, and Performance Adaptations to Four Weeks of High Intensity Sprint-Interval Training in Trained Cyclists." *International Journal of Sports Medicine* 25, 2 (2004): 92–98.

DeWeese, B. H., G. Hornsby, M. Stone, and M. H. Stone. "The Training Process: Planning for Strength-Power Training in Track and Field. Part 1: Theoretical Aspects." *Journal of Sport and Health Science* 4, 4 (December 2015): 308–317.

DeWeese, B. "The Training Process: Planning for Strength-Power Training in Track and Field. Part 2: Practical and Applied Aspects." *Journal of Sport and Health Science* 4, 4 (December 2015): 318–324.

Dicharry, J. "Kinematics and Kinetics of Gait: From Lab to Clinic." *Clinical Sports Medicine* 29, 3 (July 2010): 347–364.

Dumke, C. L., C. M. Pfaffenroth, J. M. McBride, and G. O. McCauley. "Relationship Between Muscle Strength, Power and Stiffness and Running Economy in Trained Male Runners." *International Journal of Sports and Physiological Performance* 5, 2 (June 2010): 249–261.

Farley, C. T., and O. González. "Leg Stiffness and Stride Frequency in Human Running." *Journal of Biomechanics* 29, 2 (February 1996): 181–186.

Heiderscheit, B. C., E. S. Chumanov, M. P. Michalski, C. M. Wille, and M. B. Ryan. "Effects of Step Rate Manipulation on Joint Mechanics During Running." *Medicine and Science in Sports and Exercise* 43, 2 (February 2011): 296–302.

Hoff, J., J. Helgerud, and U. Wisloff. "Maximal Strength Training Improves Work Economy in Trained Female Cross-Country Skiers." *Medicine and Science in Sports and Exercise* 31, 6 (1999): 870–877.

Iaia, F. "Speed Endurance Training Is a Powerful Stimulus for Physiological Adaptations and Performance Improvements of Athletes." *Scandinavian Journal of Medicine and Science in Sports* (October 2010): 11–23.

Lauersen, J. B., D. M. Bertelsen, and L. B. Andersen. "The Effectiveness of Exercise Interventions to Prevent Sports Injuries: A Systematic Review and Meta-analysis of Randomised Controlled Trials." *British Journal of Sports Medicine* 48, 11 (October 2013): 871–877.

Marcell, T., S. Hawkins, and R. Wiswell. "Leg Strength Declines with Advancing Age Despite Habitual Endurance Exercise in Active Older Adults." *Journal of Strength Conditioning Research* 28, 2 (February 2014): 504–513.

Mikkola, J., H. Rusko, A. Nummela, T. Pollari, and K. Häkkinen. "Concurrent Endurance and Explosive Type Strength Training Improves Neuromuscular and Anaerobic Characteristics in Young Distance Runners." *International Journal of Sports Medicine* 28, 7 (July 2007): 602–611.

Mikkola, J., V. Vesterinen, R. Taipale, B. Capostagno, K. Häkkinen, and A. Nummela. "Effect of Resistance Training Regimens on Treadmill Running and Neuromuscular Performance in Recreational Endurance Runners." *Journal of Sports Science* 29, 13 (October 2011): 1359–1371.

Paton, C. D., and W. G. Hopkins, "Combining Explosive and High-Resistance Training Improves Performance in Competitive Cyclists." *Journal of Strength and Conditioning Research* 19, 4 (2005): 826–830.

Ramírez-Campillo, R., et al. "Effects of Plyometric Training on Endurance and Explosive Strength Performance in Competitive Middle- and Long-Distance Runners." *Journal of Strength and Conditioning Research* 28, 1 (2014): 97–104.

Saunders, P. U., D. B. Pyne, R. D. Telford, and J. A. Hawley. "Factors Affecting Running Economy in Trained Distance Runners." *Sports Medicine* 34, 7 (2004): 465–485.

Schache, A. G., T. W. Dorn, G. P. Williams, N. A. Brown, and M. G. Pandy. "Lower-Limb Muscular Strategies for Increasing Running Speed." *Journal of Orthopaedic and Sports Physical Therapy* 44, 10 (October 2014): 813–824.

Sedano, S., et al. "Concurrent Training in Elite Male Runners: The Influence of Strength versus Muscular Endurance Training on Performance Outcomes." *Journal of Strength and Conditioning Research* 27, 9 (2013): 2433–2443.

Stone, M. H., K. C. Pierce, W. A. Sands, and M. E. Stone. "Weightlifting: Program Design." *Strength and Conditioning Journal* 28, 2 (April 2006): 10–17.

Spurrs, R. W., A. J. Murphy, and M. L. Watsford. "The Effect of Plyometric Training on Distance Running Performance." *European Journal of Applied Physiology* 89, 1 (March 2003): 1–7.

Støren, O., J. Helgerud, E. M. Støa, and J. Hoff. "Maximal Strength Training Improves Running Economy in Distance Runners." *Medicine and Science in Sports and Exercise* 40, 6 (June 2008): 1087–1092.

Taipale, R. S., J. Mikkola, A. Nummela, V. Vesterinen, B. Capostagno, S. Walker, D. Gitonga, W. J. Kraemer, and K. Häkkinen. "Strength Training in Endurance Runners." *International Journal of Sports Medicine* 31, 7 (July 2010): 468–476.

Weyand, P. G., R. F. Sandell, D. N. L. Prime, and M. W. Bundle. "The Biological Limits to Running Speed Are Imposed from the Ground Up." *Journal of Applied Physiology* 108, 4 (April 2010): 950–961.

Weyand, P. G., D. B. Sternlight, M. J. Bellizzi, and S. Wright. "Faster Top Running Speeds Are Achieved with Greater Ground Forces not More Rapid Leg Movements." *Journal of Applied Physiology* 89, 5 (2000): 1991–1999.

Yamamoto, L. M., R. M. Lopez, J. F. Klau, D. J. Casa, W. J. Kraemer, and C. M. Maresh. "The Effects of Resistance Training on Endurance Distance Running Performance Among Highly Trained Runners: A Systematic Review." *Journal of Strength and Conditioning Research* 22, 6 (November 2008): 2036–2044.

Index

Bolded page numbers refer to where instructions for exercises are given.

inflammation, 138, 139

injuries

    achilles tendonipathy, 140–141

    and alignment variabilities, 122

    from doing too much, too fast, too soon (TMTFTS), 130

    knee, 101

    overuse, 33, 152

    patella-femoral pain, 101

    plan for avoiding, 131–132

    and recovery, 7

    and stability, 26

    and strength training, 152

    torn ligament/meniscus, 142

    and twisting, 66

intensity

    high-intensity intervals, 200, 202

    injuries and training, 130

    performance workouts/lifts, 161, 196–197

    plyometric exercises, 178

    running, 199–200

intermuscular control, 91, 98

intermuscular coordination, 14–15, 104, 155, 156

International Olympic Committee (IOC), 136

intervals

    running, 202–203, 204

    VO2max/high-intensity, 200

intramuscular control, 91, 98

intramuscular coordination, 14

IT (iliotibial) band, 9

J

Janda, Vladimir, 101–102

joints. *See also* specific joints

    aging, 144

    balance versus imbalance, 27

    gliding and rolling action, 22–23, 24, 25, 45

    guidelines for improving mobility, 24

    load on, 5, 27

    problems, 20, 21, 24

    and proprioceptive awareness, 21–22

    sensory skill to feel position of, 20, 21

    stability around, 26–28

    stiffness, 10–11, 19, 24, 45

structure, 4

Jump Block, in power workout, 274

jumping, 135, 151, 154. *See also* plyometric training

K

kettleball exercises, 166, 167, 175, 176

Kettlebell Squat, **167**, 246, 257, 261

Kettlebell Swing, **166**, 247, 254, 263, 279

Kneeling Banded Deadlift, **112**, 241, 277

Kneeling Hip Flexor Stretch, 53, **54**

knees

    ACL tears, 22

    and alignment, 122, 123, 125, 126

    collapse, 103, 123

    injuries, 101

    kneecap release, 110

    knee complex, 105

    and overstriding, 101

    in plyometric training, 179

    tracking path of, 123, 125

L

lacrosse balls, 25, 48, 84

lactate, 200

Landmine Single-Leg Deadlift, **162**, 246, 250, 263

lateral forces, 3, 66

Lateral Hurdle Hoop, **183**, 218, 224, 228, 262

learned movements, 6, 10

learning

    motor, 26, 28–29

    and neural plasticity, 16

leg swing, 11, 36–37, 53, 99

leg turnover, 37

ligaments

    job of, 4, 142

    and proprioception, 21

    tears, 21, 142–143

load(s)

    and body weight, 2–3

    and breaking bones, 133, 134

    and forces while running, 3

    on joints, 5, 27

    and overstriding, 33, 101

gluteal, 103–104
hip, 9–10, 13–14, 103
intermuscular coordination, 14–15, 104, 155, 156–157
intramuscular coordination, 14
knee, 105
in movement system, 4
and overstriding, 101
prehab work for, 146
self-repair, 138
spinal, 59
training, 156
unplugged, 10, 13, 14, 15
weakness, 9, 14, 102, 103
muscle mass, 144, 145–146
muscle memory, 13–16, 39, 104, 196
muscle spindle, 20, 22
muscular endurance, 152
music, 17

N

nervous system, 4–5, 25. *See also* brain, the
neural plasticity, 6, 15, 16
neuromuscular training, 14, 15
new runners, 201–204, 205
Ninja Squat Jump, **181**, 216, 268
nutrition, 135, 136–137

O

optimal arousal, zone of, 17
optimal stride and form. *See* Plan A strategy
overcompensation, 9
Overhead Carry, 50, 245
overstriding, 33, 34, 36
and cadence, 37
and foot placement/footstrike, 33, 34
negative impact of, 101
pendulum swing example, 36
and posture, 44, 104
overuse injury, 33, 152

P

patella-femoral pain, 101
patellar tendon, 137
PEC Minor Stretch, **49**

pelvic crest, 124
pelvic tilt, 53, 54
pendulum-like swing, 34, 35–37, 39
performance drills, 215–216
performance power workouts
Power A workout, 272–276
Powerball workout, 281–283
Power B workout, 277–280
Performance Prep workout, 244–247
performance workouts. *See also* strength training; strength (performance) workouts
daily structure of, 197–198
frequency of, 199
length of, 197
overview, 195, 196–197
soreness from, 200
timing of, 199–200
physiological capacity, aging and, 144
Pigeon Hip Extension, **107**, 222, 226
Plan A strategy, 6, 7, 14
Plan B strategy, 6–7, 11, 14, 27–28
plank exercises
Super Swiss Side Plank, 72
Thread Needle Plank, 73
plyometric training
about, 178
for bone health, 134, 135
Box Squat Jump, 182
Burpees, 185–186
Dumbbell Push Press, 180
and force development, 155
form, 135, 179
Lateral Hurdle Hoop, 183
Ninja Squat Jump, 182
Split Box Jump, 184
strength training with, 154
technique for, 179
plyo run performance drills
Flip Flop & Push-Up Sprints, 215
Incline Sprints, 216
Stair Bounds, 216
pogo stick analogy, 154
postural control, 39, 42, 103–104, 158, 161

About the Author

Jay Dicharry is one of America's leading physical therapists and a board-certified Sports Clinical Specialist. He is known for his expertise in diagnosing and rebuilding injured endurance athletes across the globe. Having first made his reputation as an expert in biomechanical analysis as Director of the University of Virginia's SPEED Clinic, Jay blended the fields of clinical practice and engineering in an innovative way to better understand and address the causes of overuse injuries in endurance athletes. His unique approach works outside of the traditional model of therapy to correct imbalances before they affect performance and crack the code on athlete performance. He brings this expertise to numerous footwear companies as a consultant on product development, validation, and innovation.

Dicharry is the author of *Running Rewired*, Anatomy for Runners, and a regular contributor to numerous magazines and professional journals. He has been interviewed or featured in *The New York Times*, WIRED, ESPN, *Outside*, *The Atlantic*, *Runner's World*, *Competitor*, *Running Times*, *Men's Health*, *Men's Fitness*, *Shape*, *Military Times*, *Reader's Digest*, and over one hundred podcasts. He enjoys an active research career, is the cofounder and codirector of the University of Virginia Running Medicine Conference, and teaches internationally in an effort to improve the standard of care for therapists, physicians, and coaches. He's an expert consultant for industry partners to validate and innovate product. He founded MOBO as a tool to improve the foundation of athletes across the globe, and teaches at Oregon State University to develop students into the health care leaders of the future.

Dicharry is a certified coach through USA Track and Field and USA Cycling. He has coached professional and amateur athletes, ranging from local standouts to national medalists, and worked with over 50 Olympians. He has also worked closely with the US Military and USA Track and Field. Dicharry's own athletic pursuits have led him to compete nationally in swimming, triathlon, cycling, and running. These days, he enjoys exploring the outdoors on surfboards and snowboards, on foot and on wheels, savoring the days until his kids are faster than he is.